I0824489

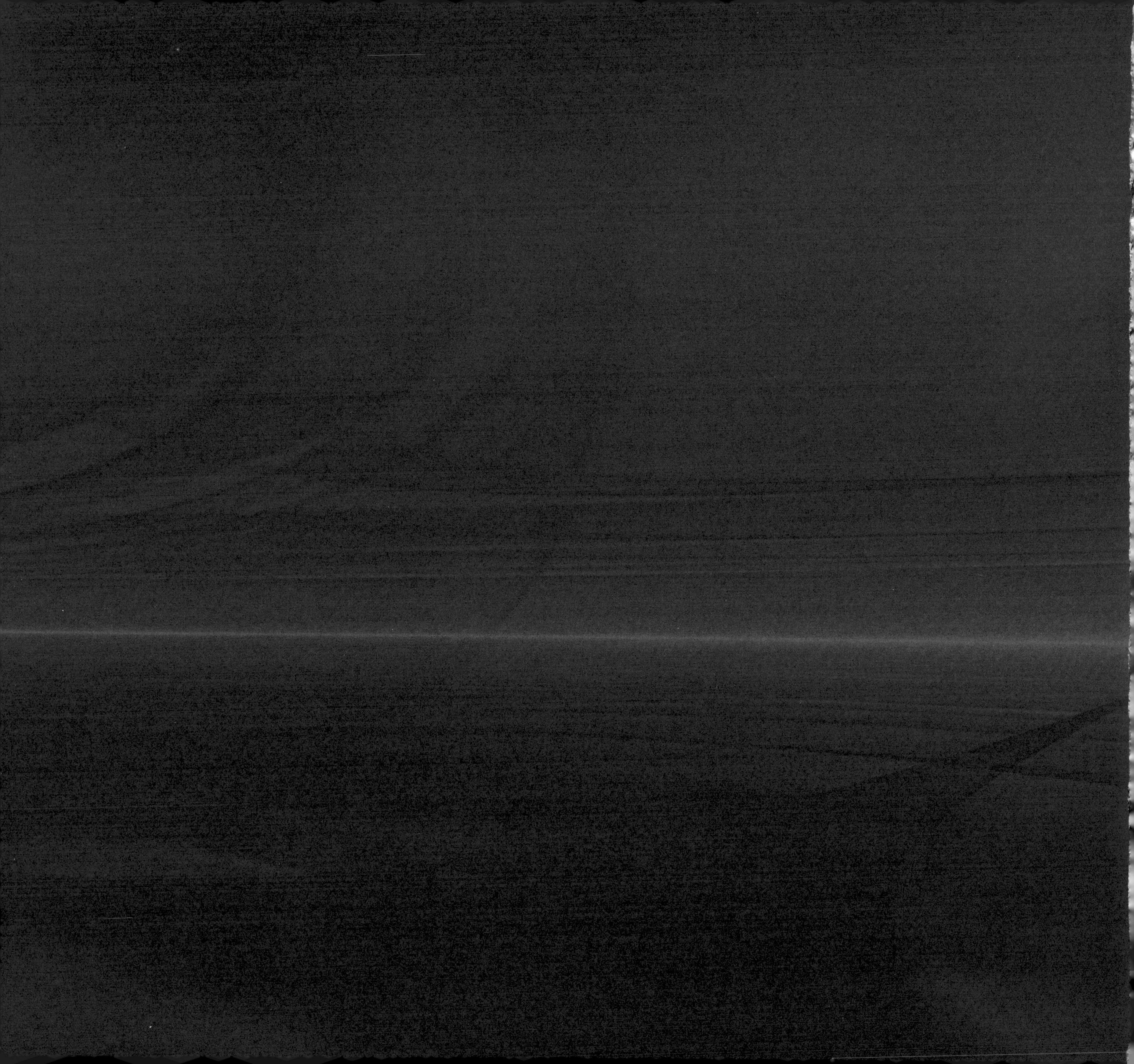

MARVEL STUDIOS
THE INFINITY SAGA

THE ART OF

BLACK PANTHER

WRITTEN BY
ELENI ROUSSOS

FOREWORD BY
RYAN COOGLER

AFTERWORD & DUSTJACKET ART BY
RYAN MEINERDING

COVER ART BY
RODNEY FUENTEBELLA

PROJECT MANAGER
ALEX SCHARF

BOOK & COVER DESIGN BY
ADAM DEL RE

BLACK PANTHER CREATED BY
STAN LEE & JACK KIRBY

TITAN BOOKS

FOR MARVEL PUBLISHING
JEFF YOUNGQUIST, Editor
SARAH SINGER, Editor, Special Projects
JEREMY WEST, Manager, Licensed Publishing
SVEN LARSEN, VP, Licensed Publishing
DAVID GABRIEL, VP, Print & Digital Publishing
C.B. CEBULSKI, Editor in Chief

FOR MARVEL STUDIOS 2018
KEVIN FEIGE, President
LOUIS D'ESPOSITO, Co-President
VICTORIA ALONSO, Executive Vice President, Visual Effects
NATE MOORE, Production & Development Executive
ZOIE NAGELHOUT, Production & Development Manager
WILL CORONA PILGRIM, Creative Director, Research & Development
RYAN POTTER, VP Business Affairs
ERIKA DENTON, Clearances Director
RANDY McGOWAN, VP Technical Operations
AXEL SCHARF, Production Asset Manager
STEPH SEMET, Digital Asset Coordinator
DAVID GRANT, Vice President, Physical Production
ALEXIS AUDITORE, Manager, Physical Assets

MARVEL STUDIOS' THE INFINITY SAGA - BLACK PANTHER: THE ART OF THE MOVIE

ISBN: 9781803368528

First edition: February 2026

10 9 8 7 6 5 4 3 2 1

Published by Titan Books
A division of Titan Publishing Group Ltd
144 Southwark St, London SE1 0UP

www.titanbooks.com

EU RP (for authorities only)
eucomply OÜ Pärnu mnt 139b-14 11317
Tallinn, Estonia
hello@eucompliancepartner.com
+3375690241

Did you enjoy this book? We love to hear from our readers. Please e-mail us at: readerfeedback@titanemail.com or write to Reader Feedback at the above address.

To receive advance information, news, competitions, and exclusive offers online, please sign up for the Titan newsletter on our website: www.titanbooks.com

A CIP catalogue record for this title is available from the British Library.

Printed in China

■ SADLER & METHOD VFX, 2-3   MEINERDING ▶

CONTENTS

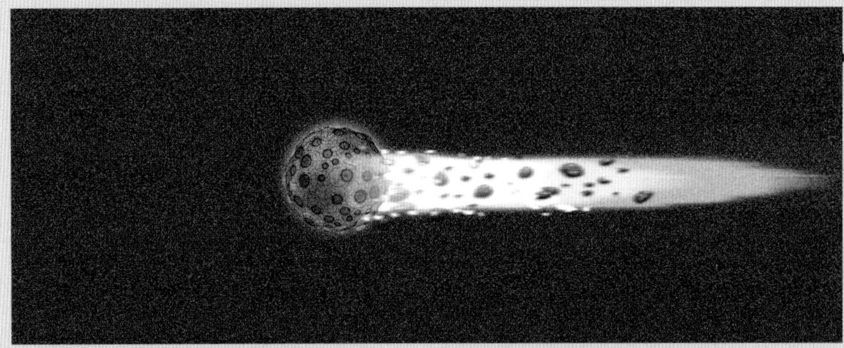

OUT OF THE SHADOWS

After a reclusive period spanning thousands of years, the African nation of WAKANDA has stepped into the spotlight, showing the rest of the world there can be a better way.

Wakanda is more than the dense jungle canopies, rich farmland, and thundering waterfalls revealed by passing satellites. Now that the once-hermetic nation has unexpectedly moved into the public arena, the people of Wakanda are swiftly showing other nations how far they've come—and how much we still have to learn.

Historically, there has been little interest from other countries in learning more about this tiny nation—a state of affairs preferred by Wakandans. For millennia, they have closed off their borders to prevent invasion by outsiders and safeguard their way of life. The world's general assumption had been that this unwillingness to engage in trade had stunted Wakanda's growth as a nation. That could not have been more wrong.

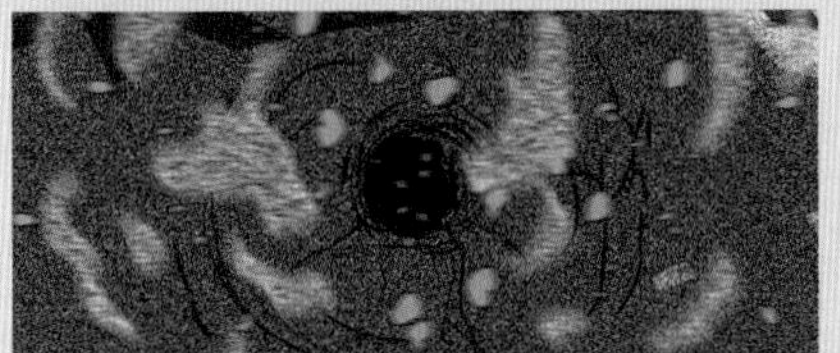

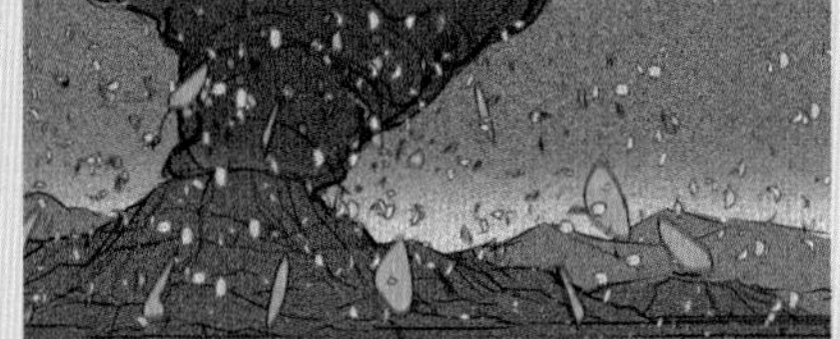

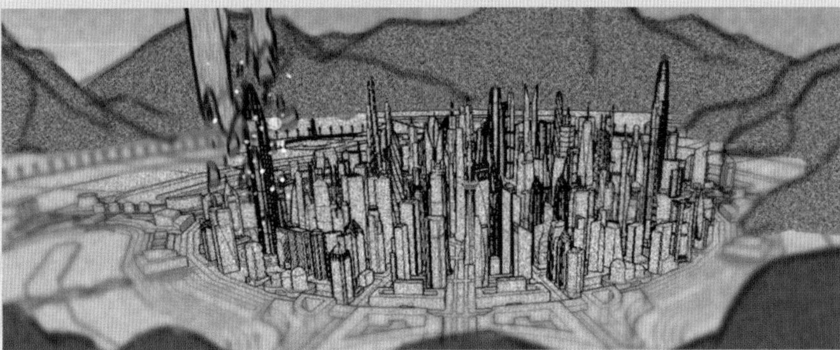

A BALANCE BETWEEN OLD AND NEW

We are in the infancy of public knowledge regarding Wakanda. As facts slowly emerge, it is impossible not to be enthralled by what is revealed. Tribal customs have been preserved, affording anthropologists a rare glimpse at traditions and ceremonies relatively unaffected by the passage of time. But these ancient traditions have not blocked their civilization's technological advancement. Wakanda's groundbreaking scientific progress far exceeds other countries' advancements in the fields of robotics, mechanics, and telecommunications.

The key to that development has been Vibranium—the rarest metal on the planet, notably used in the construction of Captain America's shield. Known locally as *Isipho*—"the Gift" in Xhosa—Vibranium is at the core of most of Wakanda's advancements.

FINDING THE STRENGTH OF THE PANTHER

When the early Wakandans discovered Vibranium, they knew they had to safeguard it from the rest of the world. To protect this valuable resource, the Black Panther was born—a mantle worn by Wakanda's strongest warrior, modeled after the Panther Goddess Bast. It is this warrior's duty to be Wakanda's protector, shielding both its Vibranium and its people from harm. While Wakanda's ruler does not always serve as both Panther and king, it is not unusual for those two people to be one and the same. From the first Black Panther—Bashenga, born 10,000 years ago—to the current incarnation, this tradition has ensured their civilization's survival.

It has not always been an easy task, but the Panther's swift action has ensured the preservation of Wakanda's secrets. Even in an age of world connectivity, it seems Wakanda's mysteries can only be revealed if its people wish them to be.

The Black Panther will forever stalk the jungles of Wakanda—both literal and concrete—guarding its gift from the world and making certain it never falls into the wrong hands.

■ **LIBERATORE**

FOREWORD 2018

by **Ryan Coogler**

What does it mean to be African? That was the question I had been wondering since before I can remember. My parents described Africa to me as best they could. I knew that although I was living in America, my ancestors came from a different place—a place far away where we assume they were free of some of the struggles that we faced as a people here in the States, until one day they were captured, enslaved, and transported thousands of miles from their homeland. But the truth was, how could I know anything about a place that I, and no one I knew, have never been?

As I got older, I came to understand that Africa was the birthplace of human life. But the representations of Africa in the media were rarely positive and always incomplete. I had learned to take great pride in my family and my neighborhoods, but the images I saw about Africa often filled me with a sense of shame. I knew these images couldn't be the whole truth about Africa. I longed to one day to go there and see it for myself.

As I got older, I fell in love with comic books. I was amazed by how characters who were told they were different could be powerful, but I was yearning for a book about a super hero who looked like me. One day, when I was still in elementary school in Oakland, California, I asked the gentleman at the counter of my favorite shop if he had any comic books about Black super heroes. He walked me over to the Marvel section and showed me the Black Panther comics. I read them, and although T'Challa looked like me, it didn't connect. He is African, I thought. I'm African-American, something different. T'Challa was the descendant of kings who knew the rituals of his ancestors by heart. I was the descendant of slaves whose true names I didn't know. T'Challa knew what it meant to be African. I only knew what it meant to be African-American.

About twenty years later, I received a call from Nate Moore, a producer at Marvel Studios who had been developing *Black Panther*. I was wrapping up postproduction on my film *Creed*, and he was finishing up work on *Captain America: Civil War*. We agreed to meet when we found ourselves less busy.

When I first sat down with Nate, I immediately found a kindred spirit. Someone who loves comics, and movies, and expects the very best out of them. Someone who found not only an escape through the genre, but also often a sense of hope and purpose.

When I sat down with Kevin Feige, Louis D'Esposito, and Victoria Alonso, I felt at ease. I knew that I had found allies who wanted to make a great movie that worked on the levels of scope, but also on emotion.

Kevin told me he wanted to bring these characters to life in a way that global audiences could connect with. He wanted his kids, who could not look more different than I or Chadwick Boseman, to see this movie and look up to T'Challa forever. I told him I wanted to make a film that explores what it means to be African, one that would have filled my 8-year-old self with a sense of pride. Thankfully for me, he and his team agreed, and we got to work immediately.

As I got ready to write the script with Joe Robert Cole, I told Nate that the first thing I would need to do was go to Africa for a research trip. The studio agreed. The trip changed my life.

I got back to Los Angeles, and Joe and I worked on the script as fast as we could. And it was then that I started the collaboration with the incredible people who were involved in bringing this film to life.

Hannah Beachler, our extraordinary production designer, understood how important this project was. She conducted major research into the visual cues and historic languages that we associate with African culture. She was able to bring about images that don't exist, channeling the Afrofuturism of Wakanda and helping to realize it on-screen. It was with Hannah that I developed a Wakandan bible, a history of Wakanda in the Marvel Cinematic Universe, detailing the history of the people and the development of their culture. Hannah led the charge in building a Wakanda that felt lived in and tactile, developing different neighborhoods and sections of the Golden City. We created a strict color story for the film, one in which we would be able to tell the characters apart.

The Visual Development team, spearheaded by Ryan Meinerding, was amazing. Ryan and his department oversaw hundreds of images and designs. I would come to love spending time with them going over different looks and iterations for T'Challa as well as the other Wakandans in the film. His team would develop keyframes, taking any random idea that I had and turning it into countless beautiful options.

Our legendary costume designer, Ruth Carter, did heavy research and tapped into her own creativity to come up with beautiful renderings for our characters. She and her team paid respect to specific tribal inspirations that we came up with while creating a look that was entirely unique at the same time.

Geoffrey Bauman, our VFX supervisor, spent countless hours bringing the world of Wakanda to life, and was patient and kind as I learned my way around these new tools and methods. Geoff studied the landscapes of the continent, and deployed several teams to take photographs of the Impenetrable Rainforest in Uganda, as well as the Rwenzori Mountains in the Democratic Republic of Congo.

To capture the images on set, I was reunited with Rachel Morrison, who I worked with on my first feature film, and who brought an amazing perspective to the project. To cut it together, I worked with Michael P. Shawver and Debbie Burman, picture editors and incredible filmmakers in their own right.

I hope you enjoy this collection of art from our collaboration.

As for the question of what it means to be African, I found the answer in this project. During my trip to the continent, I traveled and met with other African people my age, and I discovered that they were so much like me and my family back in the States that I felt completely at home. I recognized several of their rituals as things that we would do back home. I realized that for African-Americans, our African culture wasn't lost: Somehow, after all the horrible things we went through, we still found a way to hold on to it.

To be African is to be respectful of your place in nature. To be African is to love your family so much that you spend time with them every chance you get, and when your ancestors die, you never let them go. To be African is to paint the story of your people on walls of buildings, on your body, on your clothing, on the ground, and in songs. To be African means to make the most beautiful music in the world, and when it plays, to dance until you feel one with the universe. To be African means to love with your very soul, and when you fight, you fight with that, too. To be African is to be human. This project took me on a two-year journey to find an answer that was in my heart all along. For that I will always be thankful to Marvel Studios, to my *Black Panther* cast and crew, to Stan Lee, and to T'Challa.

Ryan Coogler

CREATING THE WORLD'S BIGGEST SECRET

Building the world of Wakanda, filmmakers were not just designing a country audiences had never seen before, but also an entire culture. Wakanda needed to feel authentic, just as much as the people living there—a fully functioning society with its own laws, customs, history, styles, and architecture.

"We wanted to build out the world of Wakanda because we knew that by giving the audience just the slightest glimpse at the end of *Civil War*, they'd have a lot of questions about what this place was like and what it could do and what it feels like and what it tastes like," Executive Producer Nate Moore says.

Careful planning and in-depth research, including a trip to Wakanda's home continent, were key to maintaining believability. "Going to Africa was extremely important because that's where the heart of the narrative takes place," Director Ryan Coogler says. "The fact that Wakanda exists on the continent of Africa makes it that much more complex."

"There was a lot of being mindful to make sure that I'm getting [Wakanda] right," Production Designer Hannah Beachler says, reflecting on the filmmakers' visit to South Africa. "It's so different when you're there and you can see what cities look like, what architecture of the future looks like there, and then just talking to the people and getting to know the people. So we did do some different things from what is canon to the comic, and that was a little bit of a freedom we had that was a lot of fun."

WAKANDA

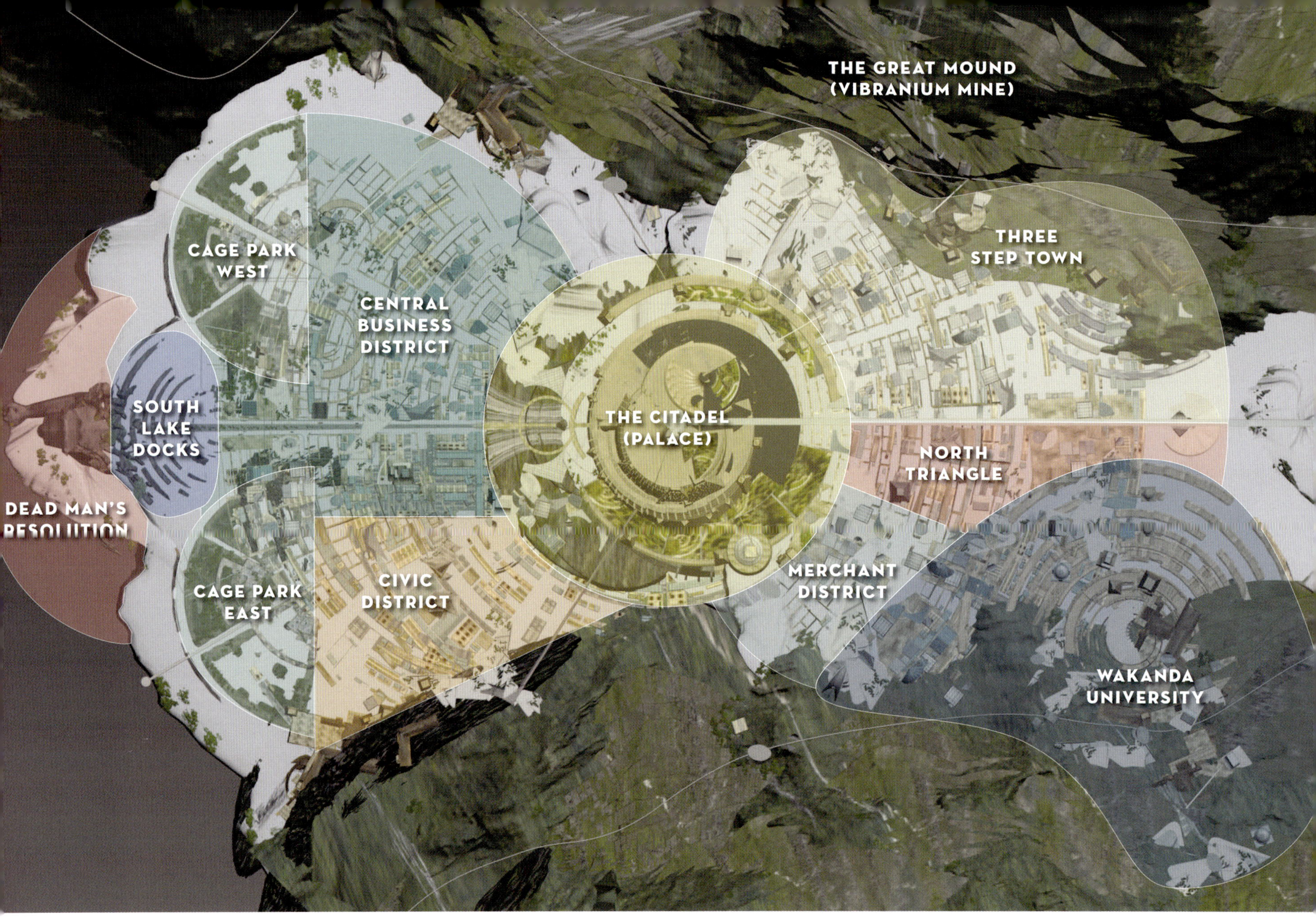

"We try to make each of these films stand apart," President of Marvel Studios and Executive Producer Kevin Feige says. "And when we get into *Black Panther*, it really is unlike anything we've done before. We are introducing a country in the middle of Africa that has been secret for centuries—pulling back those layers and going in to see it and finding a technologically advanced nation beyond anything currently on the planet. How did that happen? How did they keep their secret? What happens if that secret gets out?"

PREVIOUS NOWAK ■

BEACHLER ▲ LACEY ▶

GOLDEN CITY

The home city of the royal family and capital of Wakanda is a modern marvel, boasting a world-class university, a thriving arts scene, and a central business district. Most citizens use high-speed trains to get around, although many still choose to walk through the beautiful parks and streets. The few cars on the roads travel by levitating on magnetized paths. Thanks to continual technological breakthroughs by the Wakandan Design Group, the city is always at the forefront of modern advancement.

■ PREVIOUS **SZE**, FROM *CAPTAIN AMERICA: CIVIL WAR* ■ **NOWAK**

NOWAK

NOWAK

■ NOWAK

"Something that was really important to us was to make Wakanda feel like a place that could exist on Earth rather than some completely made-up place that was a fantasy land," Nate Moore says. "And part of that is building sets, looking for cultural references that are very real and very alive in Africa, and building that into the plot of the story. So the world of Wakanda, the idea of a kingdom, the idea of the many tribes that make up the population of Wakanda are all things that are pulled from the comics, but also pulled from the real world."

■ NOWAK

NOWAK ▲

NOWAK, DUNN-BAKER & PUI ▲

NOWAK & DUNN-BAKER ▲

NOWAK & DUNN-BAKER ▲

■ PREVIOUS SZE

NOWAK & DUNN-BAKER ▲

NOWAK & DUNN-BAKER ▲

▲ TAMM

▼ PUI

"We wanted to go after this idea of the circle of life that is in a lot of tribal cultures as far as believing that's how life begins," Production Designer Hannah Beachler says. "So that's where we went with that. And the tribal council room, we knew we wanted it to be old, and we knew we wanted it to be new. We wanted some sort of tech to enhance what is old. And a lot of what we tried to do is mix these two ideas together of our past and our present, but never getting rid of the past. It's always there.

"So with that we were like, 'Okay, well, what if there was a ruin in the middle of the room?' Some of the story that I wrote about how Wakanda came together was all the different tribe elders coming together and sitting together and talking and doing this. So they should all be on or around this ruin. And if the floor was glass we can see the ruin go all the way through this palace. And it'd be really cool because we can pick it up again when we do another set in the palace. And Ryan's like, 'You know, I really think they would be sitting on top of that ruin because everything should be tangible and touchable, and they want to constantly be living the history.' So we placed them on top. We did this glass floor, which is really high-tech-looking with all the steel that we used. And then we found an old Nigerian language called the Leopard Society, and when I discovered it I was like, 'Oh, that's perfect.' Leopard, Black Panther—it's the same. They have their own script, so we used the script on these metal columns that we lit up from behind so they look really techy. So it's this old text in this sort of high-tech setting."

■ **SZE**, EARLY UNUSED CONCEPT

"The essence of Wakanda is that they are a civilization hidden from the outside world," Concept Artist Jackson Sze says. "So how would a country that is as advanced as Wakanda be able to hide itself from everyone else? The idea [originally] was that maybe we could use a jungle canopy to hide the actual advanced civilization and architecture underneath the treetops. And that's the point of this imagery, because from a top-down view, if you were using satellite imagery or flying overhead, you wouldn't be able to tell there is an advanced civilization underneath."

WAKANDAN TRIBES

Wakanda's tribes play an integral role in maintaining the nation's survival and secrecy. Each tribe not only fulfills a specific function in Wakandan society, but also has its own distinct look. "We got Ruth Carter, who's an exceptional costume designer, working with Ryan Meinerding and the Visual Development team here at Marvel," Ryan Coogler says. "Costumes are a big part of Wakanda, a lot of our decisions come off what we're saying Wakandan culture is. We're looking at African culture. And one thing that's great about African culture is the clothing that people wear. What people put on their bodies says so much. And we are kind of leaning into that heavily. Wakanda is made up of different tribes, so we are getting into that through the clothes."

BEACHLER ▲

CHRISTENSEN ▶

LACEY ▼

▲ MANDRADJIEV

◀ ▲ LACEY

BORDER TRIBE

▲ SANCHEZ

THE BASICS: Found along the outer perimeter of Wakanda, the members of the Border Tribe appear to be simple shepherds and farmers to the rest of the world but are secretly Wakanda's first line of defense.

BASED ON: Lesotho shepherds in Lesotho, Africa

MAIN COLOR: Blue

FUN FACT: While all Border tribesmen are skilled on horseback, a select few ride rhinoceroses. Every year, in a special ceremony, young rhino calves choose a human child with whom to bond—a great honor to both the family and child selected by the animal.

RIHAL ▶

▲ KUNITAKE

W'KABI

M'Kathu is the tribe's elder, and W'Kabi is the leader of the border patrol, whose duty is to make certain no outsiders enter. "[My costume] looks really cool," actor Daniel Kaluuya says. "I've got a big blanket. It's from the [Lesotho], a southern African tribe. Basically, his hands are hidden, but then when he backs off, he's just got knives and he's war-ready. There's that duplicity of being humble and unassuming, but when the time's right—it's showtime."

W'Kabi is also a longtime friend of T'Challa. While they may disagree on Wakanda's border policy, both fiercely love their country and want to do right by it. "It's like W'Kabi is of two minds about whether to open Wakanda for Africa or whether to close it," Kaluuya says. "T'Challa wants to keep it closed."

◀ LIBERATOR

CHRISTENSEN ▶

RIVER TRIBE

▲ SANCHEZ

THE BASICS: Masters of fishing and agriculture, the River Tribe is found along the *Amanzi Kwakhona Umlambo*—the longest river in Wakanda.

BASED ON: Tsamai and Suri tribes in southwestern Ethiopia; Wagenia fishermen in the Democratic Republic of the Congo

MAIN COLOR: Green

FUN FACT: If requested by the ruler of Wakanda, they have the ability to shut down the river at various points with large Vibranium dams.

◀ LIBERATORE

Nakia's River Tribe costume was inspired by Amanirenas, the most famous of the kandakes, or Candaces. These black women warriors ruled the African kingdom of Kush for 500 years beginning in the 3rd century BC. "I was fascinated by the entire story of these independent female warriors who went to battle in a simple sheath laced with their incredible armor," Costume Designer Ruth Carter says. "Nakia's gold metallic chevrons on her chest represent the armor as well as its practical use of Wakandan Vibranium. The green color is inspired by the traditional African dress, using natural elements of leaves and flowers, of the Suri nation in Ethiopia—the same region as the Candaces. The simple green calfskin was inspired by the dress of Himba women in the Saharan region of Africa, who were fierce hunters."

Nakia, a member of the River Tribe, wearing her traditional Wakandan garb.

CHRISTENSEN

MINING TRIBE

▲ SANCHEZ

CHRISTENSEN ▶

THE BASICS: All minerals in Wakanda—not just Vibranium—are excavated by the Mining Tribe. They are generally found both living and working at the Vibranium mine in Mount Bashenga.

BASED ON: Samburu tribe in north-central Kenya; Dinka tribe in South Sudan

MAIN COLORS: Red and Orange

FUN FACT: As the threat of Vibranium theft, both foreign and domestic, is high, the tribe maintains exacting records of its use.

MERCHANT TRIBE

▲ SANCHEZ

THE BASICS: Leaders in innovation and trade, the Merchant Tribe is responsible for the manufacture and distribution of all clothing and goods in Wakanda. When conducting a trade, members of this tribe typically wear a veil to maintain anonymity.

BASED ON: Tuareg people in the Saharan and Sahelian regions

MAIN COLOR: Purple

FUN FACT: History tells us this tribe was originally two: the Merchant and Artisan tribes. The two groups merged to form the Masu, or Makers, and can often be found crafting with metal and leather, and creating various pieces of art.

▼ LIBERATORE

WARNER

JABARI TRIBE

▲ SANCHEZ

THE BASICS: Autonomous from the other Wakandan tribes, the Jabari Tribe governs itself. Found in the mountains of the Jabari-Lands, the Jabari use wood, not Vibranium, as the basis of their culture, and have become masterful carpenters after woodworking for thousands of years.
BASED ON: Karo tribe in Ethiopia; Dogon tribe in Mali
MAIN COLORS: Brown and White
FUN FACT: The Jabari is the only tribe in Wakanda that does not worship the Panther Goddess, Bast—instead worshiping the Gorilla God, Hanuman.

▲ SANCHEZ

CHRISTENSEN ▶

▼ LIBERATORE

JABARI-LANDS

Located in the high-reaching mountains of the southwest, Jabari-Lands are home to the Jabari Tribe. Having created an intricate wooden city made from the trees growing at the mountain's base, the Jabari prefer their simpler way of life—but by no means does that mean their city is any less technological, or beautiful.

▲ PUI

NOWAK ▼ ▶

NOWAK

NOWAK, EARLY UNUSED CONCEPT

■ **NOWAK**, EARLY UNUSED CONCEPT

M'BAKU

Head of the Jabari Tribe and a fierce warrior, M'Baku understands the importance of protecting Wakanda's way of life. "Like T'Challa, I am the leader of my people," actor Winston Duke says, "and I have a lot of responsibilities. And I'm worried about the future of Wakanda. My people have isolated themselves because they didn't want to be part of Wakandan society and the use of Vibranium. So for hundreds of years now, we've been living in the mountains and outside of the popular society. But now that Wakanda is potentially going to succumb to globalization and reach out to the outside world, I show up because that's a threat to everything we value, which is the old ways—tradition. And I'm worried about our future, which is real. People really value these things, and it's something that people can identify with—creating a future for your family in a way that they've known. Opening up our world is a direct threat to that, and so I challenge T'Challa for the throne.

"I like M'Baku because he also serves a really great moral function. He reminds them of their past, which is easy to forget. He reminds them of tradition, of the gods. He reminds them of service and practice. So he's laden with a lot of things that matter."

◀ ▲ STAUB

CHRISTENSEN ▶

▲ SANCHEZ

"I continued to be inspired by many things before I felt it was time to start creating the world of costumes and Wakanda," Ruth Carter says. "I was inspired first by the comics, reading the story and looking at some of the ideas that the comic-book illustrators put in the Wakandan world. I wanted to understand what fans knew about it, and the way in which the technology was visually approached. And in understanding that, I felt that I could update, because technology is continuously updating.

"I also needed to understand the Vibranium, this incredible resource they have in Wakanda—what it was and how it could be used in regards to costumes. Can they melt it down? Can they use it in jewelry? So I really needed to get an understanding from Ryan [Coogler] of what he wanted and how he wanted to see Wakanda.

"I think we've moved so far past gadgets on clothes—things that light up, and things that you could wear on your face, and things that you could wear on your clothes. Am I going to be responsible for this kind of thing? Am I going to be wiring on a top so that it has some kind of special magic? And the answer was no. I purely took it from an artistic point of view and said, 'Let's create something that hearkens from the ancient Africans and bring that into the present, and not create a style that you have never seen before, but a style that functions for them in a certain way, that features them as who they are."

SANCHEZ

ZURI

Introduced by writer Christopher Priest and artist Mark Texeira in 1998 in *Black Panther #1*, the shaman Zuri was a trusted advisor to T'Chaka and now serves T'Challa in the same capacity. "A sitting room wasn't big enough to hold the presence of him in that costume," Ruth Carter says of actor Forest Whitaker. "And we examined that, and they said, 'Is it too much?' And I said, 'Once we get him in context of the Hall of Kings, it's not going to be too much.' It had massive shoulders—there was almost like a shoulder board inside of it—so he's already this big presence, and this costume made him even larger.

"I had to kind of stay steady with what I was asked to do in terms of colors and textures because it was so complicated. The costumes were so involved with so many layers that I had to stay on one track. With regards to Zuri and the shaman costume, I stayed with the purple that Ryan deemed worthy of a wardrobe for him. And I wanted him to have a piece that was kind of spiritual and mysterious and magical. I wanted that piece to not only be traditional, but also kind of voodoo and mysterious in that way that he could create some magic or some medicine, and I worked really hard for that piece. At the challenge in the pool, he's wearing this cape over his main purple robe. His purple robe I had pleated like it's a Miyake piece—it's folded like origami."

■ BOUTTE JR.

■ BURT

BURT

"In the comics, Zuri is very big and imposing," Concept Artist Karla Ortiz says. "Most of the concepts that we did were made before an actor was cast. As such, we just tried different things to find what worked best, whether he ended up being young or old, and placed him in a variety of locations and designs. What would he look like in all leather? What would he look like in certain locations? Here he is in the city. Here he is in the jungle. And once the Dora Milaje were settled on, it really helped in forming Zuri's final design."

■ BURT

ORTIZ

"I surrounded myself with imagery from many African tribes, most notably the Maasai and Mursi tribes," Ortiz says. "Those tribes' use of natural materials—leathers, feathers, bones—incredible bead work, bright-colored cloths, and patterns all heavily inspired me as I tried to define what Zuri could look like. The final version of Zuri is much different than any of these, but in these kinds of projects the end results come after many iterations. Each iteration helps define what the final could be, and in most cases the final design ends up being a culmination of all the best ideas each painting has to offer."

■ ORTIZ

ORTIZ

LEUNG

MOUNT BASHENGA

To understand Mount Bashenga is to understand Wakanda. A meteorite consisting primarily of Vibranium collided with Earth about 2.5 million years ago at what is now Wakanda. After the tribes found the Vibranium and learned its value, they transformed the impact site into a mine where they could harvest the material for use in weapons, vehicles, clothing, and more.

■ PREVIOUS **PUI**

■ **PUI**

PREVIOUS **PUI**

LEUNG

Found deep inside Mount Bashenga is the hub of the Wakandan Design Group: Shuri's lab, where all of Wakanda's great technological advancements are made. "I always try to put a story with everything that I do because it becomes easier to understand how the design works," Hannah Beachler says. "So my story was that Shuri occupied this old space that was drilled out. There's the core down the middle of the space, and then you have this ramp that swirls up that core piece. My story behind that was that [it] was a giant drill bit at one point that was drilling down the side of the mountain and created a long time ago. Because it was so technological, it could have been 5,000 years ago, and they stopped using that type of mining. So she repurposed all of that. They didn't rip it out and take it all away—they repurposed that as part of her space. And then they went into a sort of Afro-futurist graffiti in that space, and we wanted it to feel fresh and new and not like something that you had seen before. We just wanted people to think that it was something that people could never have imagined, but also that this is super advanced."

▲ LEUNG

▲ SADLER

■ **SZE**, EARLY UNUSED CONCEPT

▶ **SZE**, EARLY UNUSED CONCEPT

▲ NOWAK

▲ NOWAK

▲ RIHAL NOWAK ▶

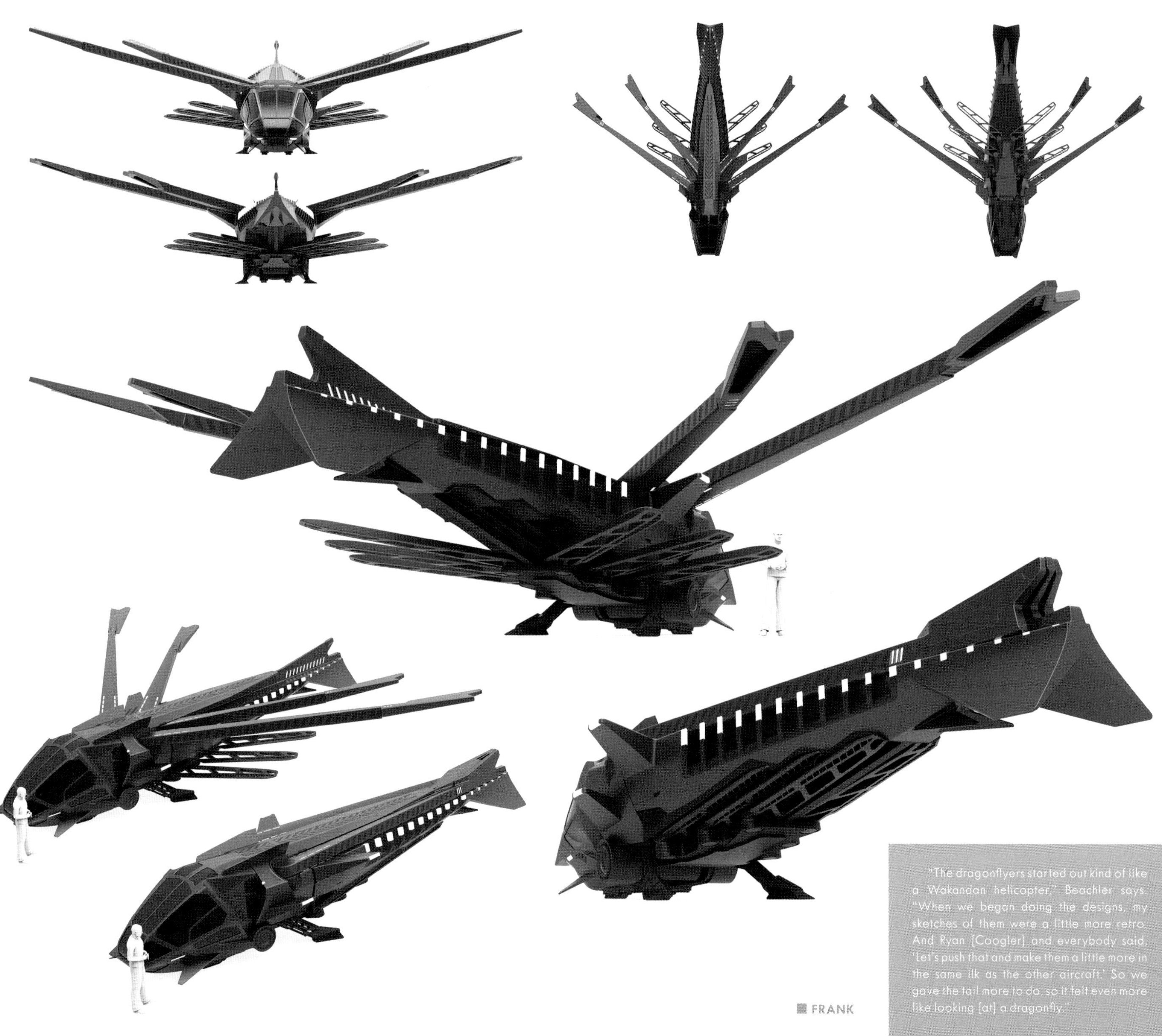

FRANK

"The dragonflyers started out kind of like a Wakandan helicopter," Beachler says. "When we began doing the designs, my sketches of them were a little more retro. And Ryan [Coogler] and everybody said, 'Let's push that and make them a little more in the same ilk as the other aircraft.' So we gave the tail more to do, so it felt even more like looking [at] a dragonfly."

FRANK

VIBRANIUM

- Mount Bashenga is named after Wakanda's first king and Black Panther.
- The ash from the original meteorite has affected much of Wakanda's flora and fauna, slightly altering their properties.
- Unrefined Vibranium has a blue glow.
- Refined Vibranium has a silvery color and complex pattern.
- Vibranium absorbs sounds directed at it. The more energy the Vibranium absorbs, the stronger it becomes.
- Alloyed Vibranium can be used in anything from cables and ropes to mesh and fabrics.

■ PREVIOUS **RIHAL**   ▲ **RIHAL**   **McCARROLL** ▶

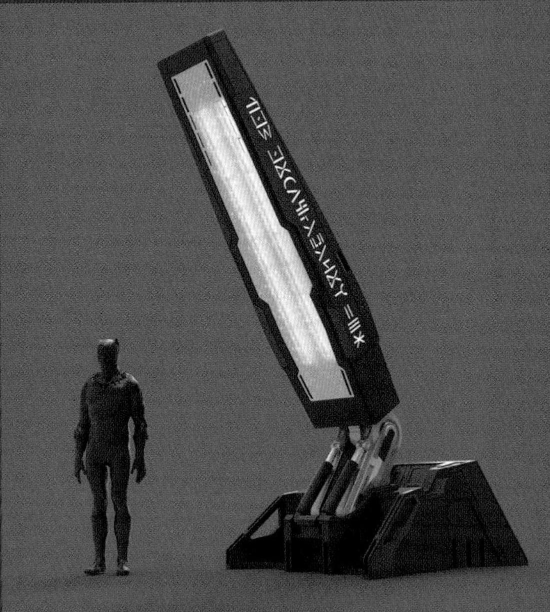

FRANK

"Vibranium's a big part of Wakanda," Nate Moore says. "It's not what makes Wakanda special, but it's how they're able to do what they do. Vibranium is the same substance that Captain America's shield is made of. But in Wakanda, they have a whole mine full of Vibranium. And so you'll get to see Vibranium used in a lot of different ways. It's a material you can build things out of. It's a power source to some degree. It allows them to have made these technological advancements.

"But what we think is really interesting is that it's the people of Wakanda that are the country's biggest resource. So as much as Vibranium and the Vibranium mine will definitely play a part in the film, it's actually the Wakandans themselves that make Wakanda a place unlike any other."

◄ METHOD VFX ▲ KUNITAKE

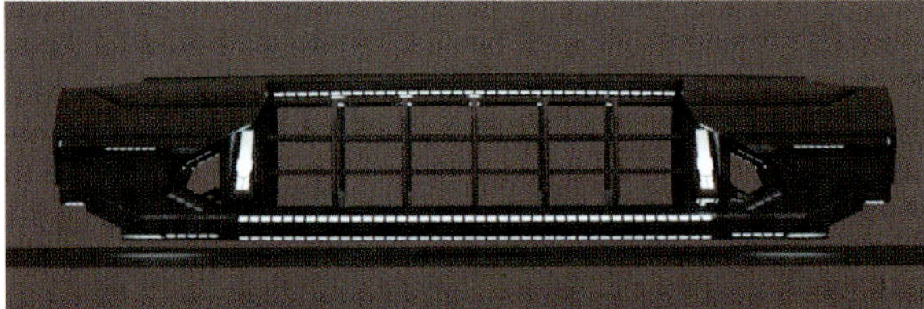
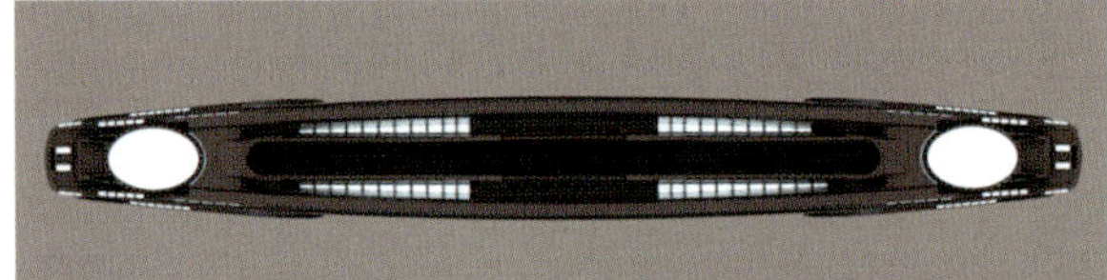
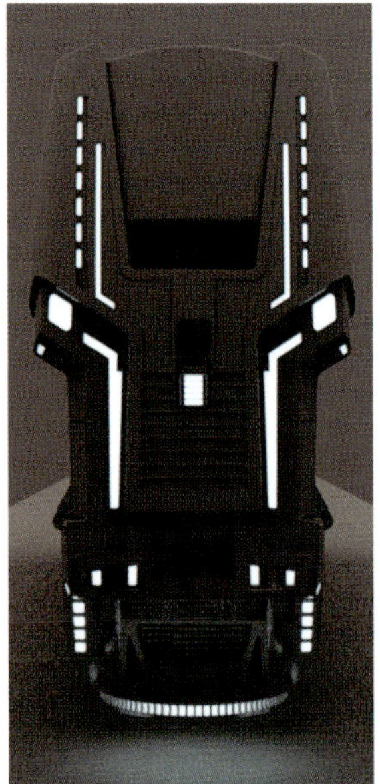

▲ HOOK

▲ McCARROLL

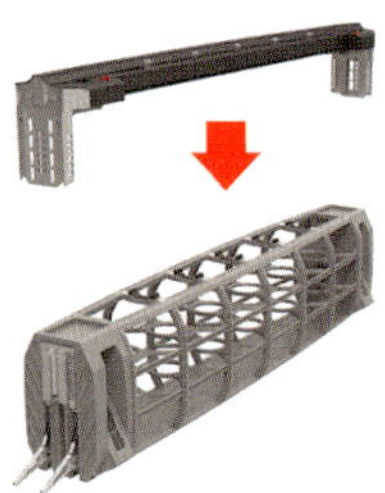

1.
CARRIAGES, PRE-LOADED WITH VIBRANIUM CANNISTERS (TBD), SIT TRACKSIDE, WAITING TO BE LOADED FOR TRANSPORT

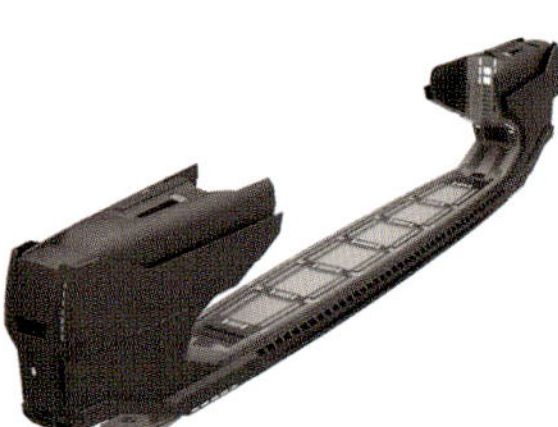

2.
ONE BY ONE, HOISTS LOWER & SLOT ONTO CARRIAGES, AKIN TO SHIPPING CONTAINERS BEING LOADED ONTO A SHIP

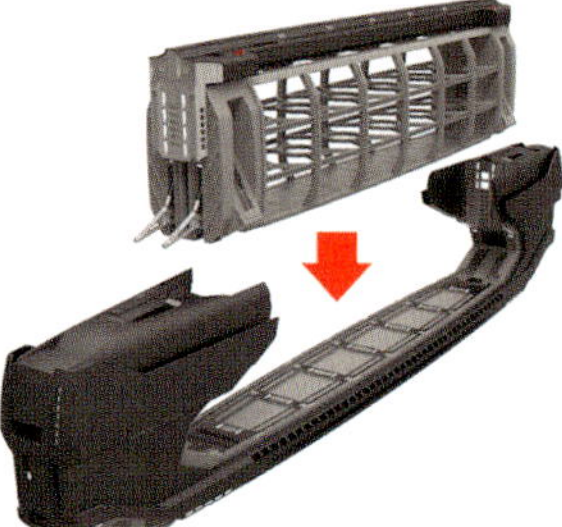

3.
EMPTY CARS WAIT ON THE TRACK, ADJACENT TO CARRIAGE STAGING AREA

4.
CARRIAGE & HOIST UNIT LIFTS & LOWERS ONTO EMPTY CAR

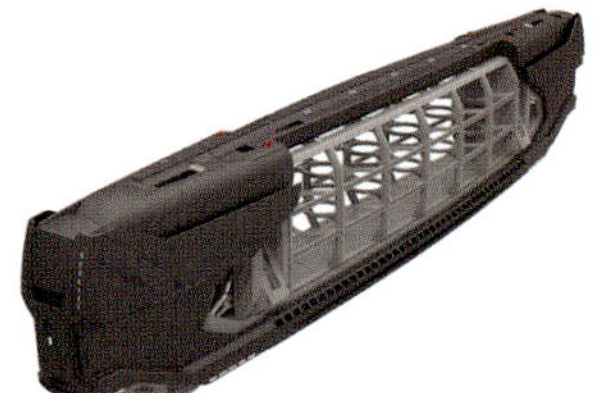

5.
CARRIAGE & HOIST UNIT SLOTS ONTO CAR FOR SEAMLESS FIT; CAR READY FOR DEPARTURE

▲ FRANK

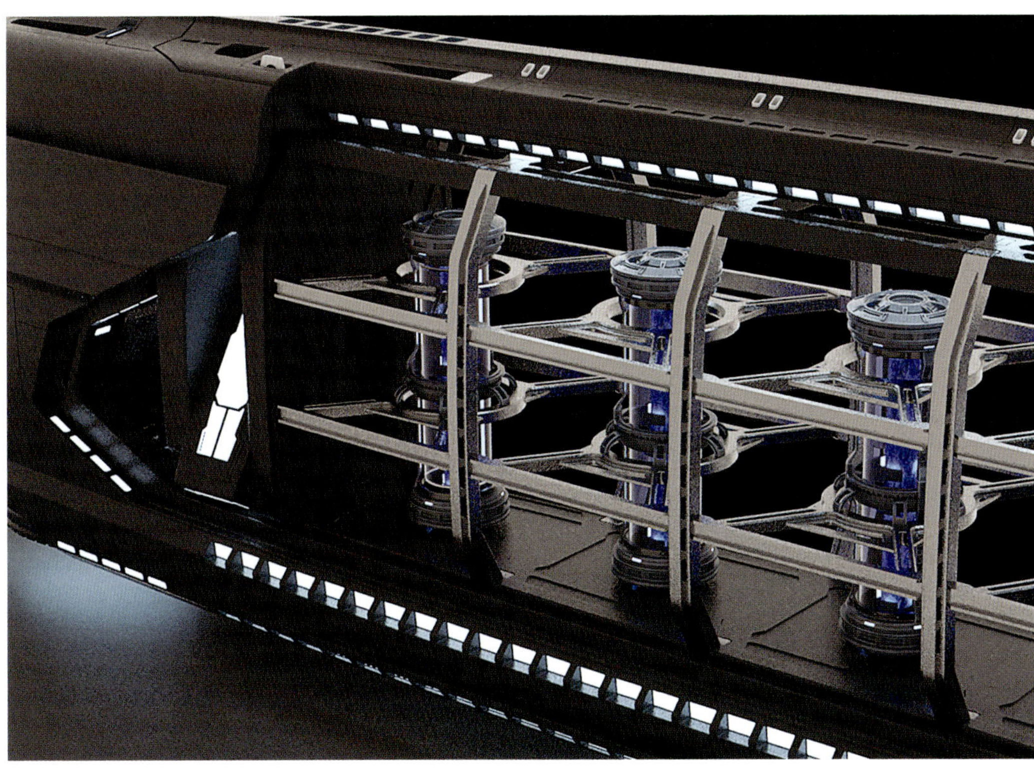

"I wanted to make sure that there was Vibranium everywhere, because it is a big deal," Hannah Beachler says. "Cap's shield is Vibranium, and we always wondered, 'What is Vibranium?' Because we've only ever seen it as Cap's shield. Well, it's kind of stainless-steel-looking to me. So let me learn about mining. Let me become a mining expert now. I did learn a lot on this. I talked to a lot of experts. What would it have to be in the beginning? And how would we get it to this point? So we could add it into the sets in different stages. You'll have to look and see what it is, what the color is, what it looks like as a rock. And then once you start to mine it, what does it look like? And once we get through all the different stages of taking away the ore and all the metallurgy of it, then we can get it to a stainless-steel look. But all the stuff in between is what we'll see in our world."

■ McCARROLL

"When you look at mining in Africa, it is a colonized situation," Beachler says. "So what would the mining be like if it weren't? That was a big question we needed to answer. We needed to figure out how [the Mining Tribe] are living, how they are transporting the Vibranium, and how they are getting back and forth to different cities. I talked to people about bringing trains to caves and different types of transportation in mines, we pieced things together and made our own beautiful, Frankenstein-type transportation and work equipment in that mine."

■ KUNITAKE

KUNITAKE

BLACK PANTHER LEGACY

DAWN OF A LEGEND

Generation after generation of Black Panthers have protected Wakanda. But while the man behind the mask has changed, his duty has not. "With Panther, he kind of exists in the gray area," Director Ryan Coogler says. "And in addition to being a soldier, he has a more important job, which is [that of] a politician. He's this guy whose world, as a monarch, is extremely complicated. And he's constantly making these choices in the fog of politics and in the fog of war."

T'Challa carries on the Panther legacy—and its burden—maintaining the balance between his responsibilities as warrior and king. "If you know *Civil War*, you know he's lost his father, and he's a prince," says actor Chadwick Boseman, who plays T'Challa. "So he's coming into the reality of what that means. Essentially, in *Civil War*, he spent the movie trying to avenge his father's death. And I think when you come into this movie, you're seeing him actually deal with the fact that he's gone and deal with the responsibility of becoming the new king, and whether or not he's worthy of that.

"Him [being] a world leader—that's a responsibility that other super heroes don't commonly have, and it's a conflict that they don't commonly have that he has to look [after] an entire nation, and then also consider that nation's place in the world and how they affect the rest of the world."

◀ TOP LEFT, BOTTOM LEFT, RIGHT CENTER, BOTTOM CENTER & TOP RIGHT **PARK**, FROM ***CAPTAIN AMERICA: CIVIL WAR***; TOP CENTER **KOVACS**; LEFT CENTER **PARK**; BOTTOM RIGHT **MEINERDING**

T'CHAKA

T'Challa is the latest in a long line of warrior-kings, dating back centuries, and a flashback sequence shows the previous Black Panther. "The idea behind the designs of what to do with T'Chaka was to create something that felt like it could be the precursor to the current Black Panther outfits," Concept Artist Rodney Fuentebella says. "Something that looked royal, less battle-ready, and more something that a stately person would wear, but still have the feel of something that we would know from Black Panther.

"In my concepts, I had the same design lines, but made him feel like the claw integration with his suit was something that was important and distinguished himself from what we know of Black Panther from *Civil War*. I wanted it to feel like it had more [of a] sense of history to it. With the cloth integration, it's how he can wear his culture around him and show he's proud of it. It's stately."

◀ MEINERDING ▲ PARK ■ PREVIOUS **KOVACS** **ROSS** ▶

"King T'Chaka was different when he was younger," says actor and Cultural Consultant Atandwa Kani, who plays young T'Chaka. "And he's more astute, more intelligent, more aware, and more caring when he's a little older. So we had to find those differences—those huge, huge differences between the way I portray T'Chaka and what happens as a consequence to my actions in that state of mind, and what happens to him afterwards."

 PARK

"I was tasked to do designs for T'Chaka, during his younger days as king of Wakanda," Concept Artist Andy Park says. "I was exploring looks that felt very classic Black Panther, but also trying to make it distinct from the modern-day look we've already seen. The idea of trying versions with his tactical vest look from the comic books was thrown out there, and I explored many variations in that direction. I also explored versions where I opened up his mask to varying degrees, since the scene might benefit from seeing the actor's face. So I did versions that showed his mouth and eyes, and a mask-less version as well.

"I thought that since this is T'Challa's father as the Black Panther, it would be cool to make him as regal as possible. So I had to try putting his classic cape from the comic book onto him. It's always fun attempting designs that harken back to the comic book."

FUENTEBELLA

"We looked at a lot of the comic reference of previous Black Panther suits, as well as where the Black Panther's suit ended up in this movie and ***Civil War***," Concept Artist Jackson Sze says. "It would definitely have to harken back to those looks. The fabric patterns would also be slightly less sophisticated because it is an older generation of the Panther suit. The body armor is actually more evident on the outside, and less a fully integrated and slim bodysuit. The addition of fabric helps to differentiate this one from the newer Black Panther suits. But also, hopefully, a rich fabric would hint at the royalty that is wearing this suit, being the king, as well as let the audience know that this is not the current Black Panther when he is on screen. There are more straps and belts and functional items that are less refined. The gold accents help to keep it aristocratic—rich and opulent and worthy of a king."

◀ SZE

■ SZE

HALL OF KINGS

Ancient and mysterious, the Hall of Kings is where Wakanda's dead leaders are buried. The domain of the priests, priestesses, and shamans of Wakanda, the Hall of Kings is one of the country's most sacred locations. At the building's center can be found the Heart-Shaped Herb, growing as it has since the beginning of the Wakandan civilization.

▲ PLANK-JORGE BUOEN ▶

If Wakanda had a national flower, it would be the Heart-Shaped Herb—a native species mutated by Vibranium in the surrounding soil. Discovered by a shaman led by the Panther Goddess, Bast, the herb grants those who consume it enhanced physical abilities—namely strength, agility, and perception. The Black Panther is the only ones allowed to ingest it.

◀ PUI
■ PREVIOUS BUOEN

▲ BUOEN
PLANK-JORGE ▶

▲ PLANK-JORGE

▲ ▶ BUOEN

▲ BUOEN & PUI

▲ KOVACS

◀ TAMM

▲KOVACS

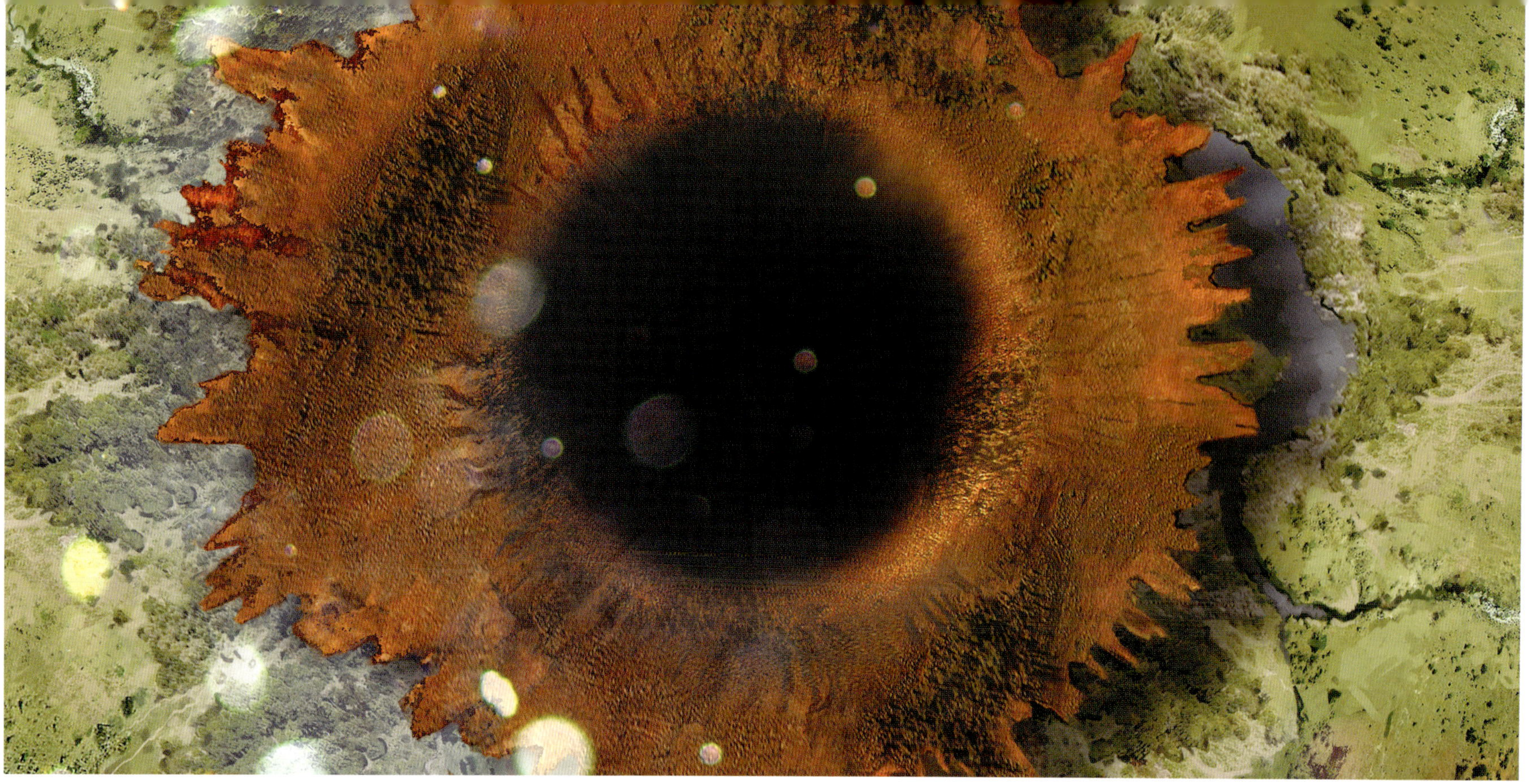

■ PREVIOUS **BUOEN** ■ **BUOEN**

After becoming king, T'Challa takes part in a traditional Wakandan ceremony enabling him to transcend to the Ancestral Plane and seek wisdom from past rulers. "That's a place where you're in an almost trancelike state, and you get to connect to your dead relatives," Executive Vice President of Physical Production and Executive Producer Victoria Alonso says. "And in this case, it's his father. He gets another chance to communicate with him. For this, we were trying to create a place that was mystical and mysterious. It's a place where you wish you could go, but it also has the tragedy of death. So there was a lot of discussion about what this place should look like. Is it dark? Is it bright? Is it colorful? I think the colors we chose are peaceful. Having an aurora borealis in the back, it's very soothing, but it also has elements of Earth to ground you in the conversation."

T'CHALLA

During diplomacy endeavors and meetings of the tribal council, the king of Wakanda wears traditional robes and other garments. "It was intimidating and challenging, and I just really wanted to get T'Challa right," Costume Designer Ruth Carter says of creating this look. "I wanted him to be relatable, as well as royal, but not over the top. With a character like T'Challa, you have to think, 'What does he look like when he's not in his Black Panther suit?' You could go so far with it, and it could be too much, and you can dial it back so that it's so simple that it's not memorable. I felt like it needed to lie somewhere in the middle, and Ryan [Coogler] was very helpful.

"Ryan is a comic-book fan, so his feelings about T'Challa were very clear. He wanted to create embroidery that was from some African pieces that he'd seen, something dashiki[-inspired]. He wanted to include that embroidery in his look. So I created his tailcoat look with these full pants, and Ryan sent me a picture that he loved to combine that dashiki-style embroidery with the tailcoat. We examined this embroidery so many ways that at times, when you thought it was perfect, you'd go to bed and wake up the next day and it looked too Asian, and then we changed it again. So it was something that was really, really, really thought-out. I'm really happy when I see images of the finished look. It really plants him there as the king with some African elegance, along with a little bit of Western influence. So I feel like it's relatable, it's different—and also, you could see the beauty in it."

■ 110-111 **KOVACS**, 112-113 **SZE** ■ **CHRISTENSEN**

GRANOV

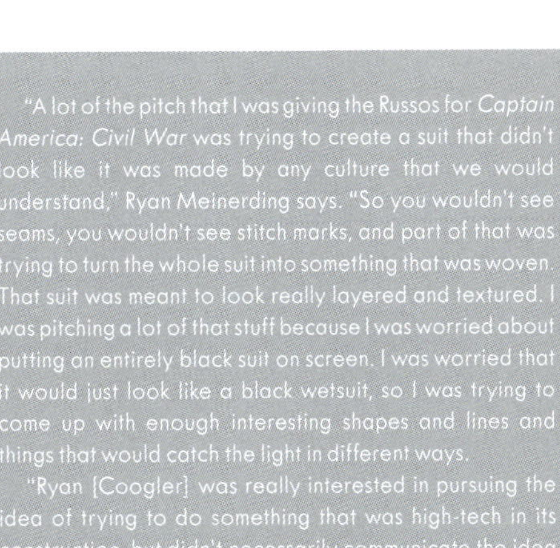

"A lot of the pitch that I was giving the Russos for *Captain America: Civil War* was trying to create a suit that didn't look like it was made by any culture that we would understand," Ryan Meinerding says. "So you wouldn't see seams, you wouldn't see stitch marks, and part of that was trying to turn the whole suit into something that was woven. That suit was meant to look really layered and textured. I was pitching a lot of that stuff because I was worried about putting an entirely black suit on screen. I was worried that it would just look like a black wetsuit, so I was trying to come up with enough interesting shapes and lines and things that would catch the light in different ways.

"Ryan [Coogler] was really interested in pursuing the idea of trying to do something that was high-tech in its construction, but didn't necessarily communicate the idea of sci-fi or technology. Ryan was really interested in turning it into a very technologically driven suit and therefore it didn't have seams, but that was because it was all one piece. And then the idea of it being a sort of nanotech suit growing from the necklace also seemed to make a singular skin suit make more sense than it having a lot of layers."

◀ SUMMERS ▲ MEINERDING

■ GRANOV

▲ GRANOV

"One of the main things that we did that was labor-intensive for this movie was trying to figure out the glow pattern of the suit," Meinerding says. "It was something that came from the Brian Stelfreeze version of the comics where, as the suit is hit, it can absorb the energy, and then Panther can use that energy—change that potential energy into kinetic energy—when he delivers a punch or a kick."

"We tried to come up with something that looked like tribal tattoos," Concept Artist Adi Granov says. "Someone in the studio came up with this Wakandan alphabet, so I tried to then incorporate those symbols into it. It went back and forth between Ryan [Meinerding] and I, because he did quite a lot of that glow. Because the suit is so textured—it's almost like a mesh on top of a mesh—my idea was to actually have the light-up stuff, the energy, inside that mesh so it's coming through. I always thought it was a cool idea that it's not just magically lighting up, but there is actually something inside the suit."

◀ SUMMERS

SUMMERS ▶

GRANOV

GRANOV

◀ DEMARTINI

■ MEINERDING

◀ NIZZI

■ NIZZI

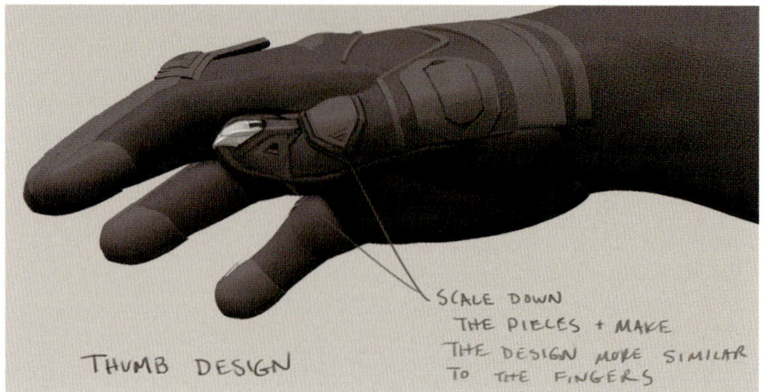

▲ **MEINERDING,** FROM *CAPTAIN AMERICA: CIVIL WAR*

◀ **PARK,** FROM *CAPTAIN AMERICA: CIVIL WAR*

▲ **MEINERDING,** FROM *CAPTAIN AMERICA: CIVIL WAR*

"The ears on Panther are traditionally pointing upwards, but Brian Stelfreeze flattened them and pointed them back in his version in the comics—I think to try to hint at more of an angry-cat look," Meinerding says. "Stelfreeze also did some really interesting things with the face where it felt like a mix of a man and a panther, and it could kind of feel more like a cat or more like a man depending on the lighting and shadows. Ryan [Coogler] really wanted to take the cat parts of that and work it into the mask that we were working on."

■ MEINERDING

■ MARANTZ

"[Black Panther] is unique as a super hero," Vice President of Marvel Studios Louis D'Esposito explains. "He not only has superpowers, but he's also the king of the most technologically advanced country on planet Earth."

"What was so exciting coming out of [*Captain America: Civil War*] was seeing audiences respond to the new characters that we introduced for the very first time. And the character that really popped out of that movie was of course the Black Panther, a character that's been a staple of Marvel Comics for years and finally gets his big-screen debut—and does so in a way where he steals the limelight from Iron Man and from Captain America. People came out of that movie going, 'I want to know more about that character, I want to see more about his world.' And that, of course, is exactly what we're doing in the Black Panther feature. It's been a long time coming, and we think the setup for him from *Civil War* was perfect. So now we get to design the world of Wakanda, see Panther's lineage, see Panther's other outfits, meet the amazing, rich cast of characters that surrounds him, and really do an entire movie that focuses on the repercussions of *Civil War*—[seeing] how that then goes into the sort of geopolitics of Wakanda—and put together a cast and a crew that is among the best that we've ever assembled," says Kevin Feige, President of Marvel Studios and Executive Producer

MARANTZ

BURT

■ ORTIZ

◀ SUMMERS ▲ GRANOV

GRANOV ▶

"Ryan [Meinerding] said the director was really leaning toward Brian Stelfreeze's look from the comics," Granov says. "So my first take was to try to find that—to take the silhouette of that and try to movie-fy it and make it a bit more realistic."

▲ SUMMERS

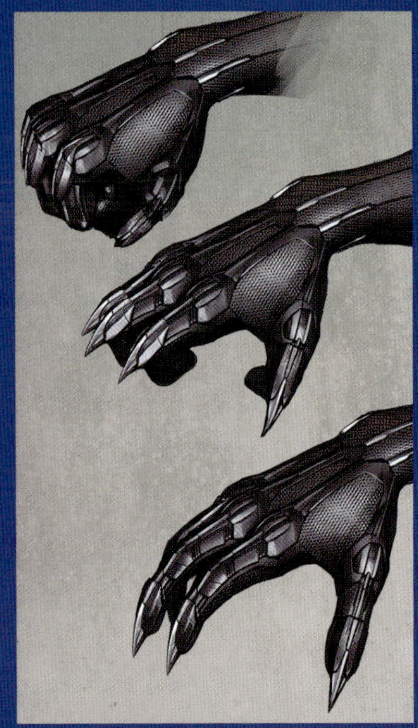

▲ GRANOV

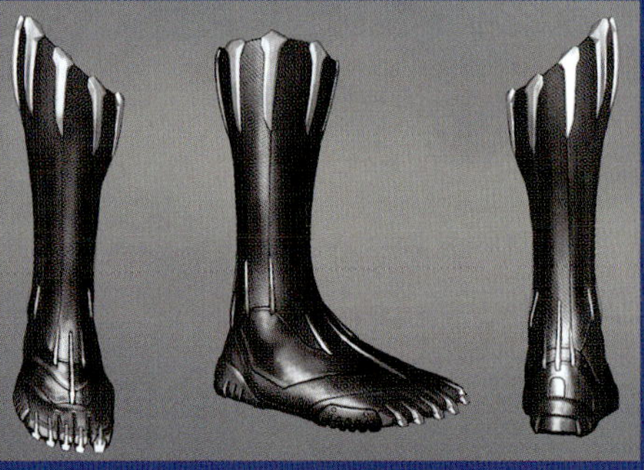

▲ GRANOV

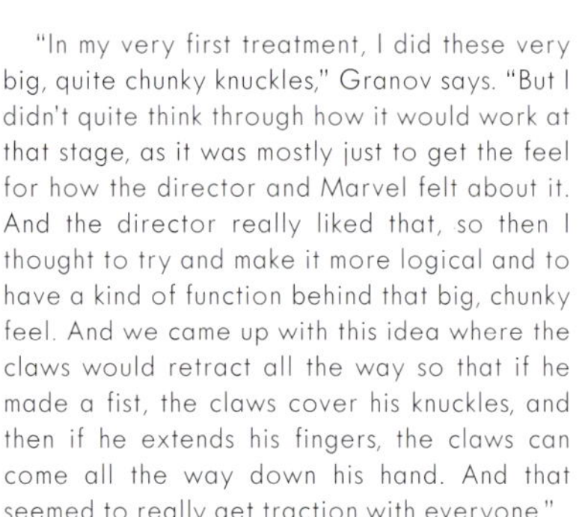

"In my very first treatment, I did these very big, quite chunky knuckles," Granov says. "But I didn't quite think through how it would work at that stage, as it was mostly just to get the feel for how the director and Marvel felt about it. And the director really liked that, so then I thought to try and make it more logical and to have a kind of function behind that big, chunky feel. And we came up with this idea where the claws would retract all the way so that if he made a fist, the claws cover his knuckles, and then if he extends his fingers, the claws can come all the way down his hand. And that seemed to really get traction with everyone."

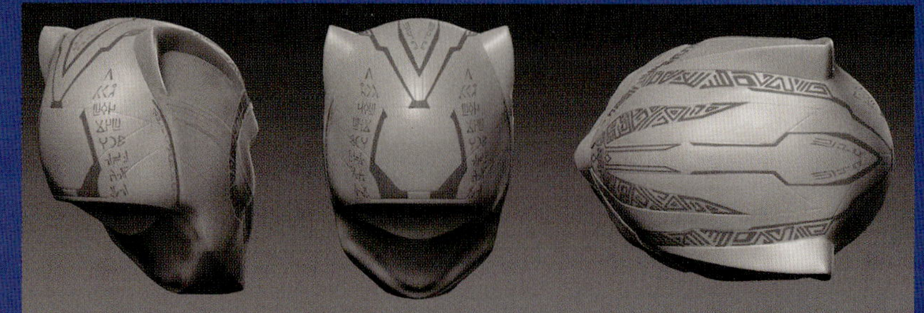

▲ ROSS & SUMMERS

"I worked very closely with Ryan Meinerding on realizing Adi Granov's helmet illustration in 3-D," Concept Artist Tully Summers says. "I used a head scan of Chadwick as a base to ensure that the forms and angles we wanted to achieve could actually be worn. We went through many iterations exploring repeating layers of woven material, alternating smooth surfaces with coarse types of patterning and symbols, and variations on sheen and specularity. There were a few experiments with the idea that the helmet's ears could change shape and articulate with the Panther's mood. A lot of effort was spent on ensuring Chadwick had enough space to see and still convey emotion with his own eyes, while maintaining the forms and angles that made the helmet iconic. After the final form and materiality was achieved, there was a second design pass adding the Vibranium trim and highlights, then a third incorporating the kinetic glow patterns."

■ **SUMMERS**

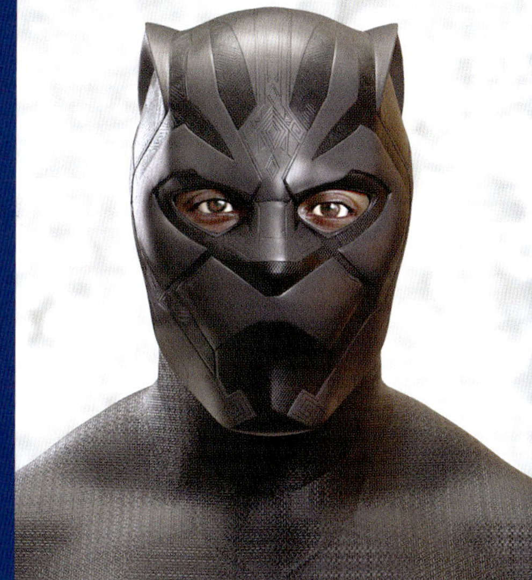

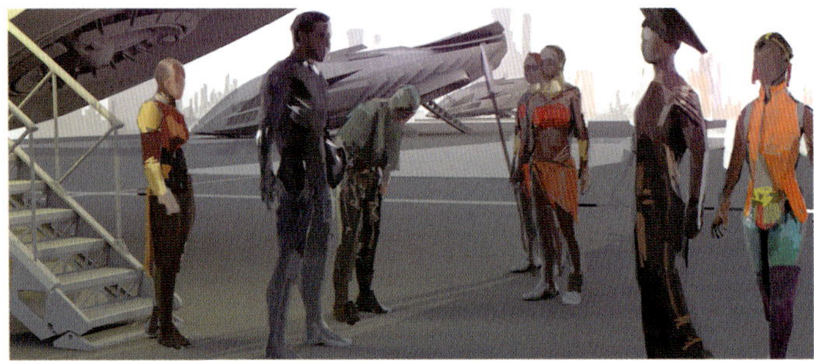

THE ROYAL TALON FIGHTER

T'Challa arrives home in the Royal Talon Fighter under different circumstances than when he left Wakanda. With his father's death, he must take on a role he did not expect to fill so soon. "The Art Department did a lot of really great illustrations on what Wakanda looked like, so I used that as a jumping-off point," Rodney Fuentebella says. "But from there, I wanted to create a sense of royalty and importance. This is when Black Panther first comes home—knowing that his dad has died and he is the new king, and wondering how they would welcome him back, and him first meeting the queen again, his mom, and how that would play out. So I looked at a lot of different movies—how they would compose royal shots, and how you would see royalty engage each other. I wanted to have this very symmetrical feel where it felt very strong, and how Black Panther is stationed in the middle and he's lit from behind and you have a sense of him carrying a burden. That is how I would interpret that feel into the composition by having it feel very weighty, but strong at the same time. The Wakandan buildings and the ships and everything are around him and support him, but at the same time weigh him down."

FUENTEBELLA

◀ ▲NOWAK ▼PUI ▲NOWAK ▼PUI

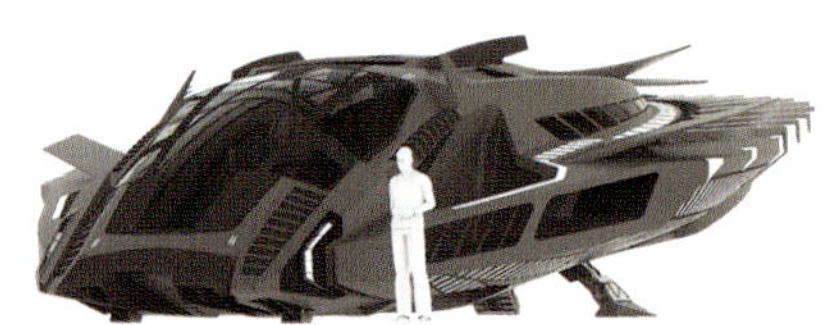

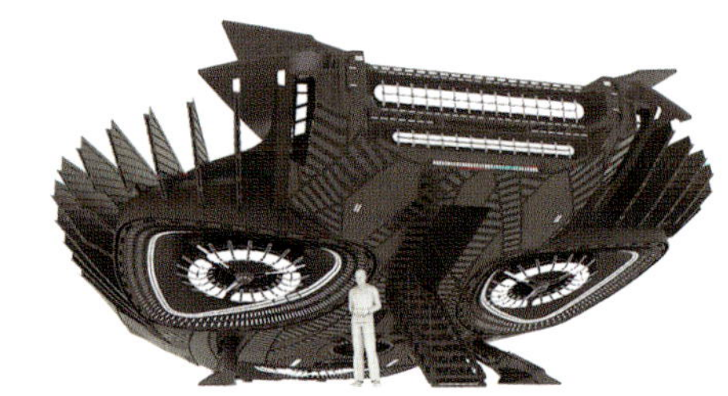

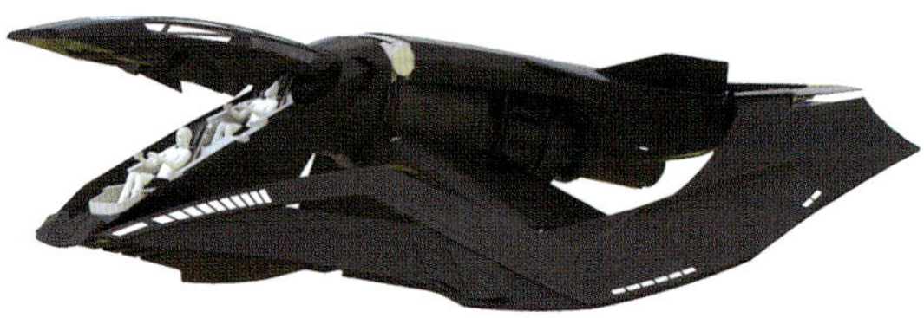

FLIGHT POSITION
FUSELAGE LOCKED DOWN
WINGS FLATTENED
CANOPY & CONSOLES LOWERED
SEATS FULLY RETRACTED

TAKEOFF POSITION
FUSELAGE PARTIALLY FLATTEN
WINGS ROTATE UP
CANOPY & CONSOLES LOWER
SEATS RETRACT

LANDED POSITION
FUSELAGE FOLDED
WINGS LOWERED (AS LANDING GEAR)
CANOPY & CONSOLES RAISED
SEATS EXTENDED

HIURA

"This is comparable to Air Force One," Beachler says. "It's T'Challa's specific aircraft that is flown by the *Dora Milaje*. We wanted it to be something that you hadn't seen before, but we wanted it to also feel familiar on the interior. We didn't want it to be like a spaceship because they're not in space, but we wanted it to feel like a very luxurious aircraft that has all of the bells and whistles that Vibranium can give it. But how they feel about their technology is that it's not a luxury. It's just something that they have. So it's super different. When we first started developing it, we presented Ryan [Coogler] two different ones. And one was based on the peafowl. And then I thought we should do one based on an African mask, and see how everybody feels about it. And so we kind of went from there, and the response was resounding in the direction of the mask."

TALON FIGHTER (MASK)

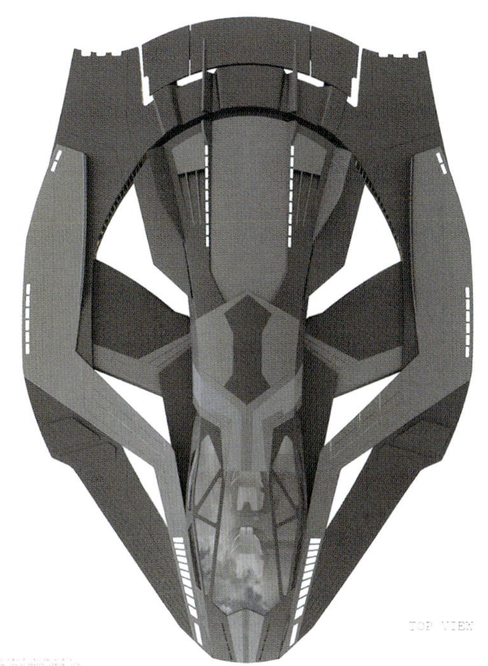

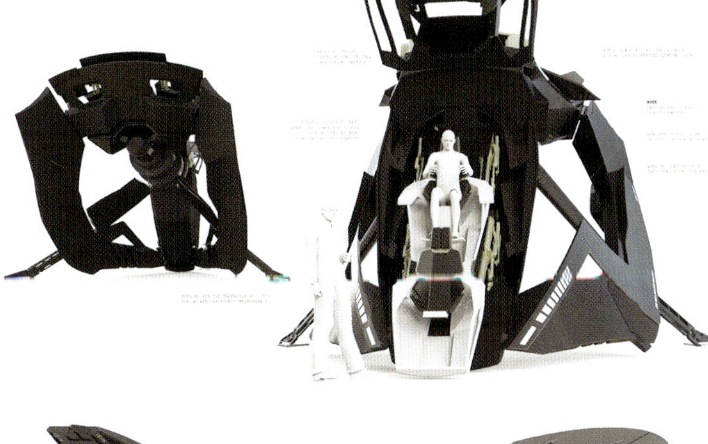

FRANK

▲ KUNITAKE

■ 146-147 **MANDRADJIEV**, 148-149 **LE**

◀ **MANDRADJIEV** **LE** ▶

"When creating these keyframes, I was inspired a lot by National Geographic images of jaguars, pumas on trees, and stuff like that—and also by the original ***Predator***," Concept Artist Alex Mandradjiev says. "I kept hearing Alan Silvestri's bongo drums from ***Predator*** while painting those images in the jungle. There's one where he is standing on a tree trunk and another where he's in the background stalking the enemy."

JACKSON SZE '11

■ **MEINERDING**

■ 152-155, 158-159 **MANDRADJIEV**; 156-157 **SZE**

WARRIOR WOMEN OF WAKANDA

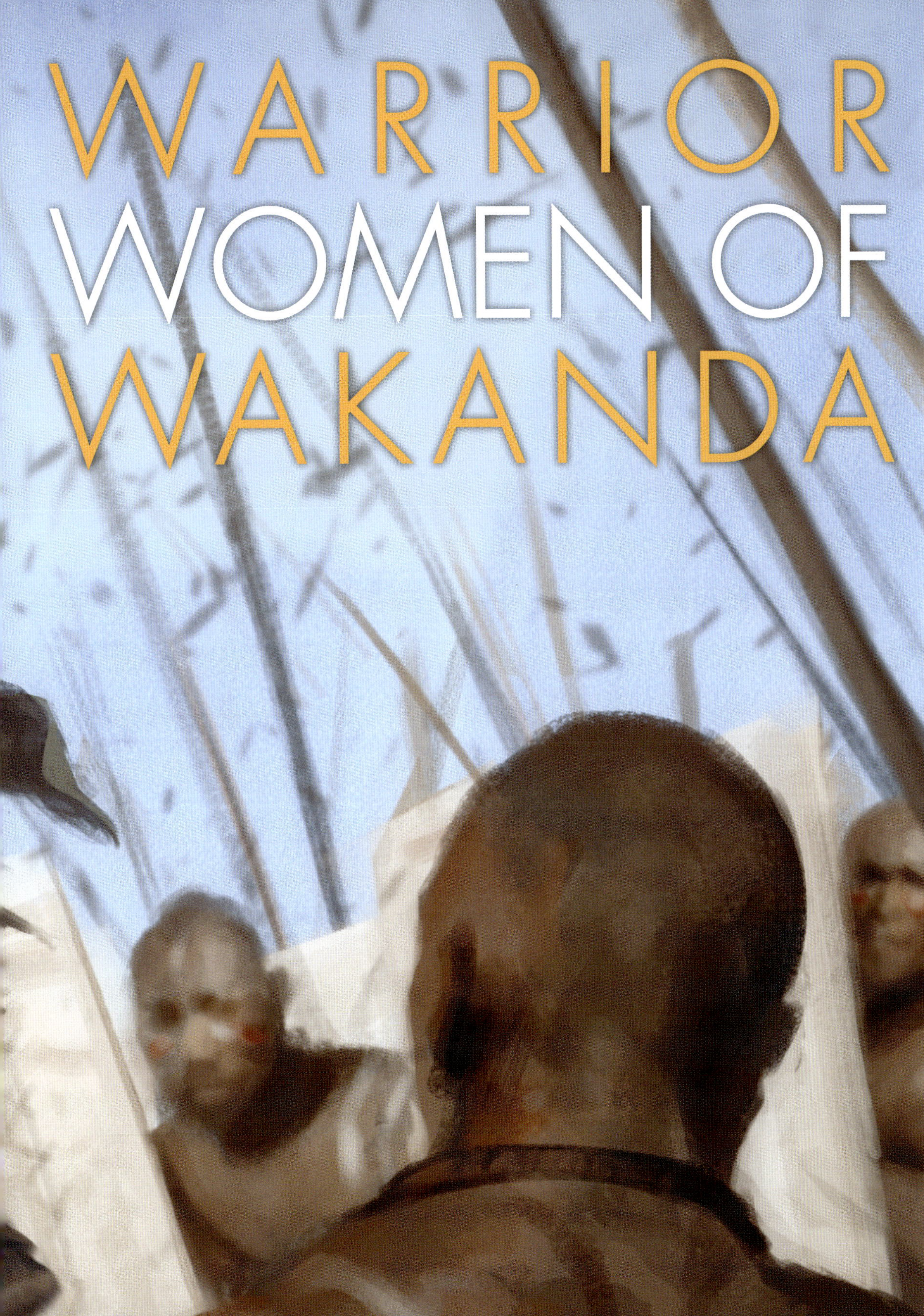

WOMEN OF THE TRIBES UNITE

Among the tribes of Wakanda are countless powerful and formidable warriors—perhaps none more so than the *Dora Milaje,* the nation's premier fighting force. Imposing in both stature and strength, the Adored Ones are not only the Black Panther's personal bodyguards, but also Wakanda's special-operations force. "I thought [the script] really brought to light beautiful components of women from the African context of the power of this very unseen kingdom," says actor Danai Gurira, who plays *Dora Milaje* leader Okoye. "It's this sort of notion that I think a lot of folks who are from the continent love.

"We have women from all over the world. A lot of these women are stuntwomen; a couple of them are dancers. It's so interesting to bring all these women together and have us work like this. And I don't think that ever happens, you know? You don't really see that, where we're brought together to create an army. And we all have to shave our heads. And so, of course, instantly it's a sisterhood where everyone has a shaved head. It's been really cool."

"The *Dora Milaje* are the fiercest warriors that defend Wakanda," Executive Vice President of Physical Production and Executive Producer Victoria Alonso says. "And whether it's them, or Nakia, or Okoye, or the Queen Mother, or even Shuri with her capacity to fight not hand-to-hand—although she gets a chance to do that—but with technology, they very much speak to where we are today in our world. I think that they're a very exciting representation of women in our super-hero movies that we haven't had very many of. We've had one or two here and there, but [these ladies] are full-on. The women of Wakanda are the hardest line to cross. If you're going to cross this country, you'll have to face them—and I don't recommend it."

◀ ORTIZ

DORA MILAJE

Just as lionesses are a pride's fiercest hunters, the *Dora Milaje*—composed entirely of women—is Wakanda's premier military force. Similar to the U.S. Navy SEALS or the UK's Special Boat Service, these female fighters are the best in the business—and as deadly as they come. "The idea for the costume's tabard came from my childhood—tribal stuff and patterning from Filipino decorations and table runners that I used to see when I was younger with my grandmas and older aunts," Concept Artist Anthony Francisco says. "I think that's why when designing this stuff, I was really into it, because I could pull from the indigenous tribes from the Philippines. There is this tribe—the Ifugao. It's from their costume that I got some inspiration from Philippine heritage and culture."

Details of the warriors' costumes were tailored to help denote hierarchy. "In this image, you can see Okoye has a gold armor piece, and Nakia's is silver," Francisco says. "This was to help symbolize the rank. Think of it as modular, the chest pieces and the legs and everything else accessorizing them to make them fit the rank. The one who has the silver is at a lower level and is not as skilled of a fighter, so she would need more armor to cover her body. The other woman, her armor is smaller and lighter because she's very good at moving and she doesn't get hit as much."

For the big screen, the *Dora Milaje* costumes needed to combine beauty with function, as combat is the force's primary task. To underscore the importance of legacy, the design also integrates an item of cultural significance.

"There is a piece in front of the *Dora Milaje* costume, the harness, and I really wanted that piece to have meaning," Costume Designer Ruth E. Carter says. "The *Dora Milaje* are the toughest fighting troupe—they protect the king, and they're the highest-ranking military in Wakanda, and they're all women. So if you are accepted, or asked to be a part of the *Dora Milaje*–I put it in terms of today–if that were to happen, if someone in your family was in it, you would be very proud of it, and want to show it, too. 'My grandmother was a *Dora Milaje*, and that's why I'm working to be a *Dora Milaje*.' I'm seeing that being handed down from previous generations like a family heirloom. So, I was thinking, 'What part of this costume could be something that a young *Dora Milaje* would be proud of to have handed down from their grandmother, or their mother?' And it's the harness."

■ FRANCISCO

ORTIZ

ORTIZ

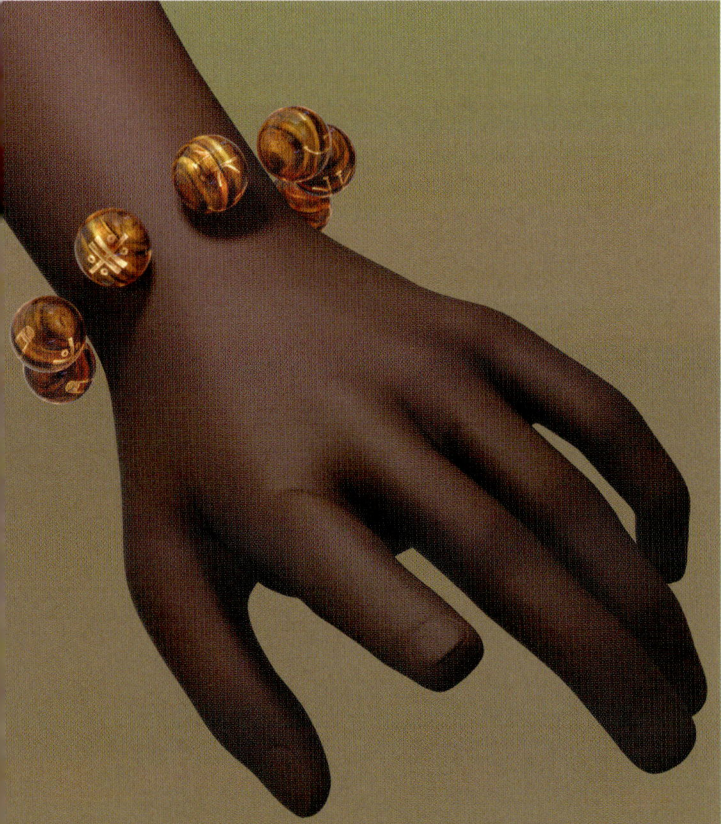

"The Kimoyo Beads are from the comic books," Property Master Drew Petrotta says. "They're basically a computer that you wear on your wrist like an ultra-modern version of the iPhone. Each person has a prime bead that they are given at birth that is a bit of the ancestral bead, and the other beads have Wakandan symbols on them, made out of Vibranium, and you can use them like a computer. Each bead has at least four different characters on it, and the original idea was that you could spin the bead to create sentences to have the beads do what it is you want them to do, as if typing into your phone.

"Shuri's beads are a little bit more technologically advanced than the rest of the society's, as she's the lead scientist for Wakanda. That's how she controls the vehicles—with a bead, or a version of a bead."

◼ JOYNER

KOVACS ▶

OKOYE

"Okoye is the head of the *Dora Milaje*," Executive Producer Nate Moore says. "With the exception of the Black Panther, she is the best fighter in the nation. So with that comes a sense of dignity and respect from the rest of Wakanda because she really is their James Bond to some degree.

"What we think is interesting about Okoye is that she has an almost sibling relationship with T'Challa. Because they train together [and] work together, there's a real friendship there between a man and a woman that is not romantic at all, but has the depth of any other friendship you've had in real life—which is something that we don't always get to play with in the Marvel Universe. Also, because the role is the best fighter in Wakanda, there is a ton of cool physical stuff we get to do with Danai."

■ PREVIOUS **SZE**

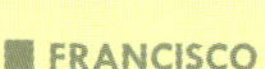

■ **FRANCISCO**

ORTIZ

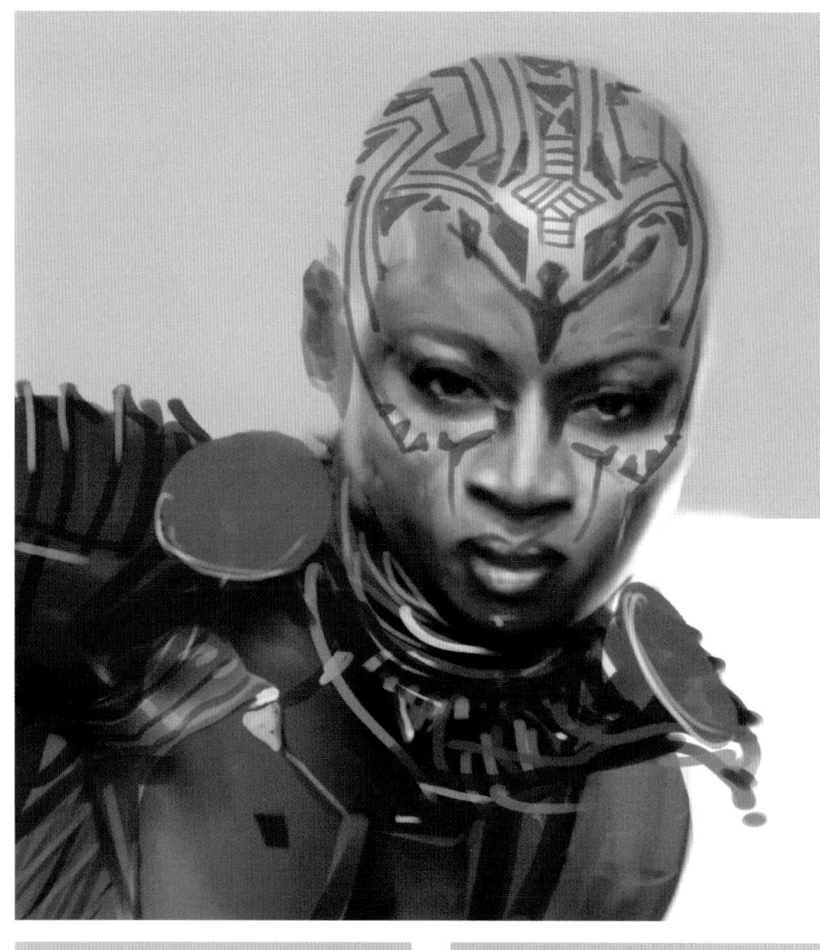

■ FRANCISCO

CHRISTENSEN

"The director originally wanted something to cover the faces of the ***Dora Milaje*** to offer them some more protective armor," Concept Artist Karla Ortiz says. "I looked to many different locations around Africa to help inspire their design, but I ended up focusing primarily on Morocco. The design concept ultimately wasn't used in the final costume, but they did end up using elements of it for other characters in the film. It's always great when that happens."

■ JOYNER ORTIZ ▶

FRANCISCO

"The idea for this spear is that it is formed using nanotechnology, like liquid Vibranium or something," Anthony Francisco says. "When the two bracers on the arm are aligned, the spear would start to form outside of the bracers, and eventually they would be long enough to connect. So she would have to have her hand straight, it connects, and she could pop out the fully formed spear into the air and grab it. That's why it's on the center of the arm. In the end, they didn't use this transformation mechanic for the film, but they still liked the design of the spear."

■ FRANCISCO

NAKIA

"Lupita [Nyong'o] is playing a character named Nakia, who's got a very close, personal relationship with T'Challa that dates back to when they were really young," Director Ryan Coogler says. "Their relationship is complicated, circumstantially. And they both are involved with the Wakandan military."

Nakia is a War Dog—Wakandan spies sent to observe other countries and report back to their homeland. In this role, she has proven herself not only as skilled in surveillance, but also as a skilled fighter.

FRANCISCO

■ FRANCISCO

■ FRANCISCO

ORTIZ

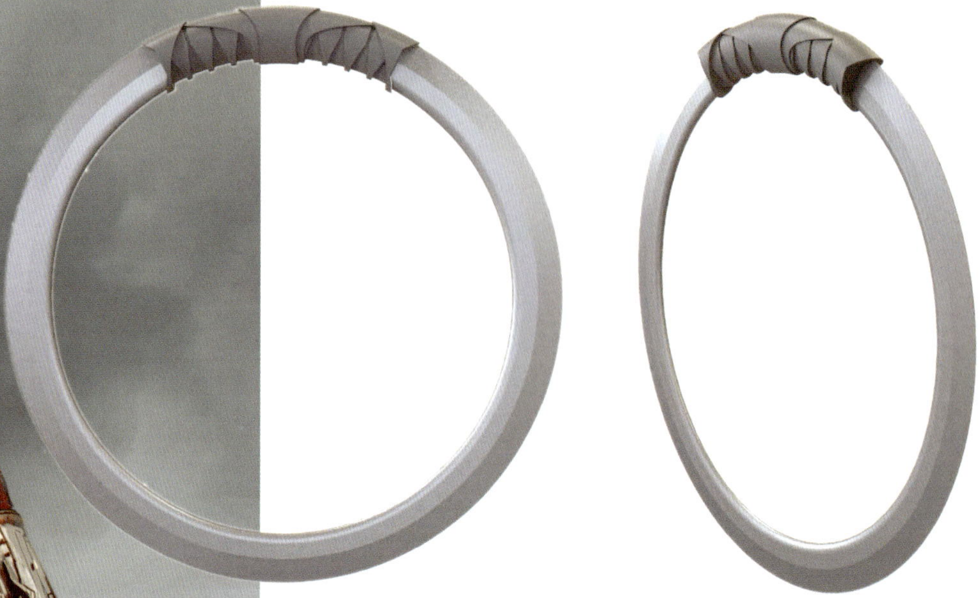

▲ ARTIST

Nakia's weapon of choice is her rings. Made of Vibranium, they can be used up close in slashing movements, or thrown in a way similar to the chakram created and battle-tested by the Sikhs and the Rajput from India. However, Nakia's rings represent a new take on tribal weaponry. "I wanted to try to come up with something different than what everyone thinks a tribesperson would have, which is a spear," Anthony Francisco says. "Obviously, it could be a high-tech spear, but I wanted something more, and just different. I did a little circle thing that felt like a boomerang, and then I was thinking of the weapon in terms of game design: what's the special ability, and can she throw this, and if so how fast would it be if thrown, would it have projectiles? And knowing she should be able to attack in both close combat and long range, the entire design just came together."

"Anthony's solution for Nakia's weapons—he came up with that by himself," Head of Marvel Visual Development Ryan Meinerding says. "They're a lot of fun. The idea of rings floating inside of the larger rings that are electromagnetically suspended, and then those being able to fly out and hit people—I think that's pretty rad."

◀ FRANCISCO

CHRISTENSEN ▶

RAMONDA

Ramonda is the Queen Mother, matriarch to all of Wakanda, and her costume was used to help separate her visually from the rest of the country's citizens. "If you are queen, what do your clothes look like? And how intricate will you be able to design your costume as queen?" Ruth Carter says. "It wasn't so set in one particular way. Like, 'This is how Wakanda looks.' It was a little bit more of a forward approach to fashion and utilizing all of the technology that we have today, and putting it in clothes in a way that people haven't seen. And so the queen's costume was 3-D printed in Belgium, and it was African lace, but it was scanned into a computer and algorithms were created to form this shape that we printed out with a special material that was flexible. And when it came out, it wasn't a hard, plastic toy—it was actually a garment. Her hat, which was also 3-D printed in Belgium the same way—is shaped like hats worn by the Zulu tribe, because these pieces that she's wearing had to tell a story in and of themselves. It makes it more meaningful to have it made out of another material and done in a different way."

"Ruth Carter, the costume designer—some of her renderings and sketches, they are beautiful," actress Angela Bassett says. "Or some of the inspiration that she's taking, they're really quite beautiful. I trust that she can get me there. It's all about putting all of that on. A lot of that tells the story, and it just feeds from the outside, which will feed the inside."

■ CHRISTENSEN

SHURI

They say age is just a number, and the Black Panther's younger sister, Shuri, proves just that as head of the Wakandan Design Group. "Shuri is T'Challa's little sister and also a young girl who's very ambitious," actress Letitia Wright says. "And she's very intelligent and innovative. She's always creating stuff and advancing Wakanda—the technology and everything. She helps to develop so many of the things that are going to be helping her brother along his way.

"What I've connected with is a sense that she's ambitious. She wants things for the right reasons, and I can connect with that. She's a positive spirit, and I love that. I try to carry that wherever I go—just be positive in everything. When she opens her mouth, then you're like, 'Whoa, this kid has wisdom. She has understanding.' That's someone I'm trying to be, and trying to grow into as a young woman. When you speak to her and you see what she does with her talents, you have to take a step back and go, 'Okay, this kid is really cool.'"

■ SEKERIS

▲ CHRISTENSEN

"Shuri, design-wise, was a mix between the Black Panther costume and the *Dora Milaje*," Karla Ortiz says. "She's a young girl, so it was very important to not have her be seen in a sexual way. Her body is covered more than what most audiences tend to expect of female characters in super-hero movies."

"How much do we play up her feminism vs. her scientific approach to everything? Because she's very smart, she's very gadgety," Concept Artist Constantine Sekeris says. "Like Peter Parker, she's a brain and she invents things. She has these gauntlets as well. She's a scientist. So we try to play with that, mixing in technology with her costumes so she can be youthful and fun.

"Early on, we started with something very formfitting, very sci-fi, and then it evolved into 'Let's try to add something a bit more tribal, and now something a bit more royal with more patterning and a color palette of blues and blacks mixed in with a bit of gold.'"

ORTIZ ▲ ▶

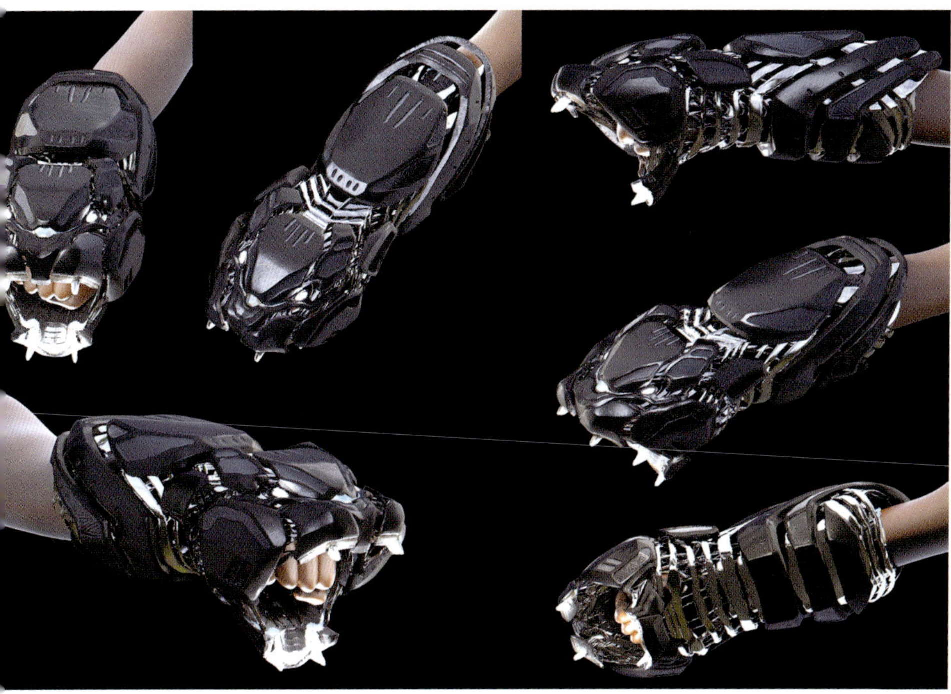

▲SEKERIS

"I started designing Shuri as a whole," Concept Artist Tully Summers says. "My earliest design was a scaled-back Black Panther suit with Vibranium power lines running down her arms to her blasting panther heads. I then introduced more earth-toned natural cloth to scale back on the high-tech black, as it was a little too on the nose and left very little visual arc. Shuri's costume remained very close to my early takes. I had a lot of fun 'deconstructing' that look into her ritual version she wears at Warrior Falls."

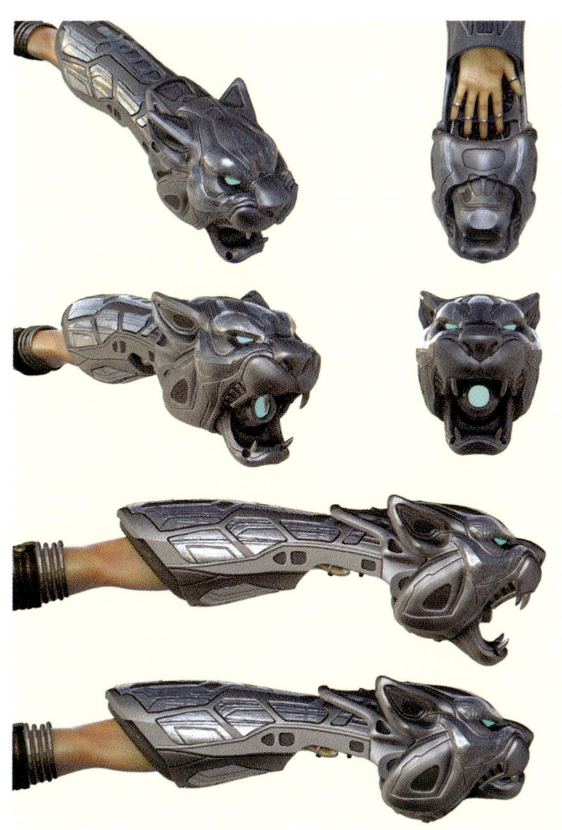

◄ ORTIZ

SUMMERS ► ►

SUMMERS

■ SUMMERS

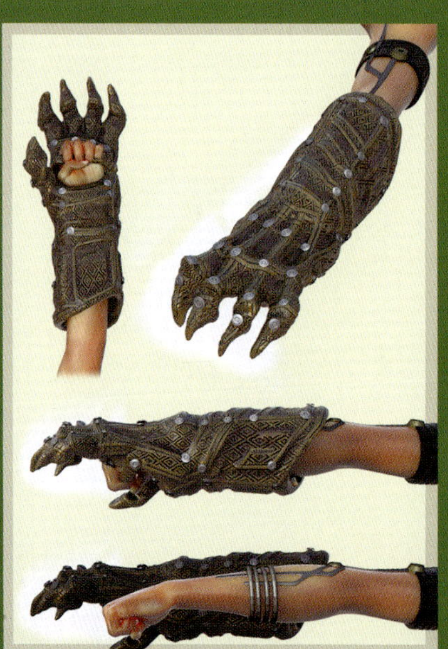

Although ultimately adopting a panther-head design, Shuri's gauntlets initially were inspired by a different part of the cat. "There was some vacillation on whether her gauntlets should start out as claws and then progress to blasters, and whether they were static or articulated with her own fingers," Summers says. "I explored all those variations. Constantine Sekeris eventually landed on the cool blasters that snap open in the film."

■ SUMMERS

■ SUMMERS

■ SUMMERS

■ SEKERIS

■ SEKERIS

▲ LEUNG

TAMM ▶

"When we were first coming up with things for Shuri's lab, we wanted her to have an interface," Production Designer Hannah Beachler says. "And we knew what Tony Stark's interfaces looked like, and I was totally against doing a hologram, because that's what we see all the time. And if Wakanda is advanced, they have to go beyond the hologram. We're talking about technology that doesn't exist yet.

"So, I went back to the sand created [from the Vibranium-mining process], and I said, 'What if they made this sand technological?' If we're in the Vibranium mine, and they're extracting this Vibranium, the rock melts away around it, and when it melts it becomes like lava sand. So, our sand is going to be black, and it's going to be almost like nanites. Shuri's whole [lab] floor has a bunch of these sandboxes. When she makes the Lexus for the car chase in Korea, the sandbox frame drops and the extra sand drops, but it leaves the shape of a car—a car that you can get in and drive."

◀ LEUNG

THREATS TO WAKANDA

PREVENTING EXPOSURE ON THE WORLD STAGE

When Wakanda's mysteries are imperiled, it is the Black Panther's duty to quell those threats by whatever means necessary—whether in costume or undercover. "What's interesting about the film is that Wakanda is a secret nation to some degree: People know that it exists, but they don't quite know the expanse of the nation," Executive Producer Nate Moore says. "A lot of our heroes aren't going to know what's going on until it's too late to help. So what you find is a character, in the *Black Panther,* who is trying to stop a threat to his country without allowing that threat to become public—because he knows as soon as it becomes public, Wakanda all of a sudden will find itself in the crosshairs. So it has a very underground-thriller tone to it. It's not open warfare on a global scale. It's something that feels a little bit more clandestine than that."

Waging this secret war on Wakanda are Ulysses Klaue—first seen in *Avengers: Age of Ultron*—and Erik Killmonger. Both characters are aware of Wakanda's secrets, but the latter possesses an insider's knowledge of the country. "I think Killmonger is a big threat to T'Challa because he truly understands Wakanda," Director Ryan Coogler says. "They say if you know your enemy, then you're in pretty good shape. It makes you very formidable. It's really a film about what society has come to. It's come to information, right? And when it comes to information, it's those who have it and those who don't. And above all else, that's what Killmonger has."

KILLMONGER

Anyone who knows of Wakanda's mysteries is considered dangerous, earning Killmonger a spot on a short list of people capable of ruining the charade played out to the world by the Wakandans. "Erik Killmonger is somebody from the comics whom we've talked about for a lot of years," Nate Moore says. "He is sort of the main adversary to the Black Panther, and he's someone with his own idea of how Wakanda should work. So here is this fictional African nation that's the most advanced nation in the world, yet is secluded and has cloistered itself from the rest of the world, and that's something that T'Challa as the new king plans to keep carrying on. Well, Erik Killmonger has a very different idea of how Wakanda should be positioned in the world and how they should use their resources, both technologically and financially, to change the way the world works. And I think that tension betweentwo men who have two varying degrees of opinions as to how Wakanda works is what the film is built around."

Killmonger's background informed his look. "We wanted to have this idea of Killmonger being this renegade soldier who had ties with Wakanda, but had severed them," Concept Artist Rodney Fuentebella says. "I wanted his outfit to have a very military feel with his combat vest, but have it where it has a sense of history and culture to it. So for the designs I did, I wanted to reflect this African and Wakandan culture with integration of the patterns and the detailing, but first and foremost have a very combat-ready feel."

■ PREVIOUS **SZE** ■ **FUENTEBELLA**

■ FUENTEBELLA

FUENTEBELLA

■ SUMMERS

▲ SUMMERS

FUENTEBELLA ▼ ▶

"For Killmonger's tribal mask, I definitely tried to create something that was a little dark and intimidating, while also being something that had a lot of history to it," Fuentebella says. "It also needed to be something that I thought the character of Killmonger would be drawn toward, because he does take it. So it needed to fit his personality and what he felt like he could embody. The designs I did had more of an animalistic, demon-type vibe to [them], which would be something that would intimidate anybody in front of him. Ultimately, Tully [Summers] was the one who came up with the really cool final design.

"Killmonger's mask was intended to evoke fear," Concept Artist Tully Summers says. "I explored versions that were deteriorated, hinting at decay, various demonic silhouettes, and horns—all trying to achieve a tribal boogeyman."

▲ ORTIZ

▲ ORTIZ

FUENTEBELLA ▲

◀ ORTIZ ▲FUENTEBELLA

◀ ▲ ORTIZ

"We spent a lot of time doing the designs of [Killmonger's] scarification," Rodney Fuentebella says. "That was something that was very important, so a bunch of us did a lot of takes on his scarification and tried to come up with something that he could do himself that shows different types of patterns and how he would do it—if it would be chaotic, or if it would be very systematic."

Concept Artist Karla Ortiz took a hands-on approach—literally—to her designs. "I'm a very bendy person," Oritz says. "So by looking in a mirror, I knew that every place I could reach, Killmonger would also be able to reach and place the tattoo scars. That helped me know what would be possible, or not."

▲ SUMMERS

▲ FUENTEBELLA

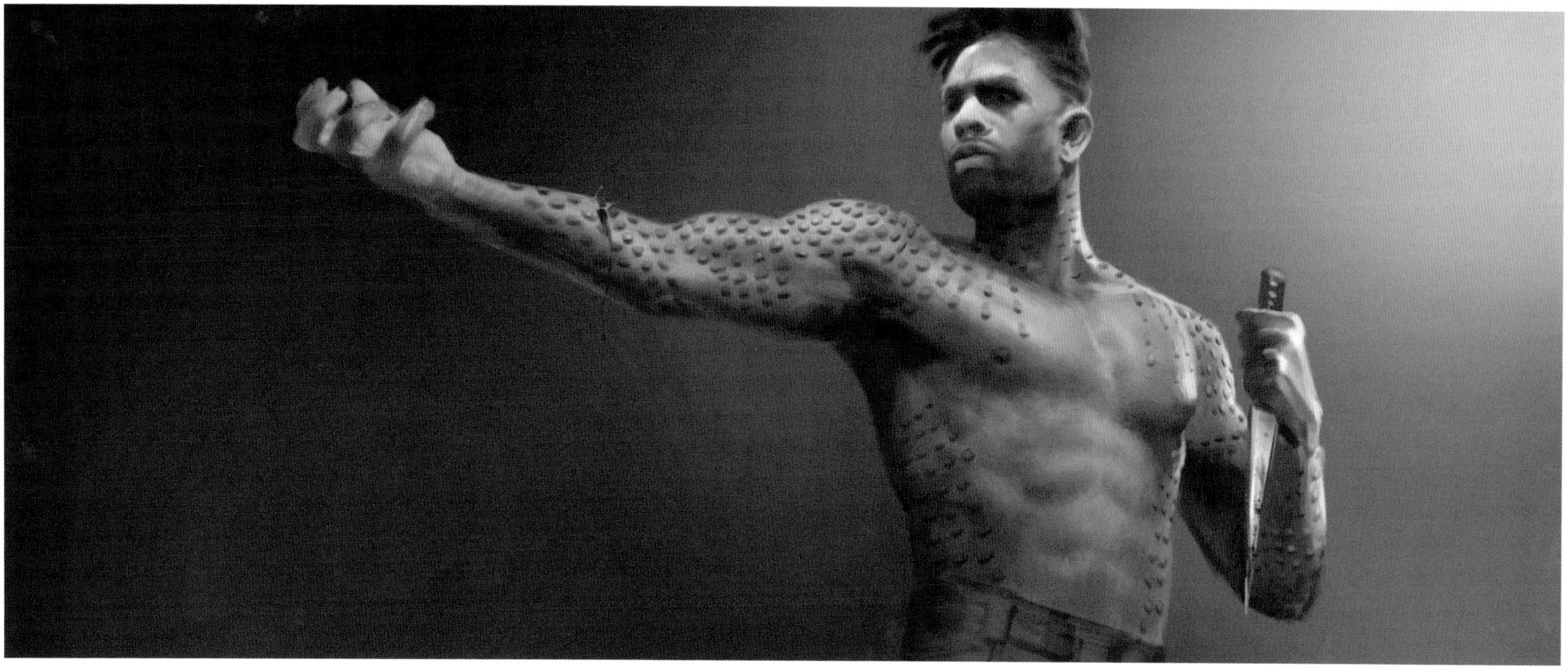

PREVIOUS **FUENTEBELLA**

ORTIZ

McCAIG

KLAUE

Once an enemy of Wakanda, always an enemy of Wakanda: Black-market arms dealer Ulysses Klaue once stole millions of dollars' worth of Vibranium from the country and lived to tell the tale, and he remains Public Enemy No. 1 in the eyes of Wakandans. Last seen in *Avengers: Age of Ultron* getting his arm ripped off by the film's titular villain, he has since received a new one—with some deadly features.

"The idea of these was to create something that felt very different from what we have seen before, different than the Iron Man stuff and more menacing," Rodney Fuentebella says. "So that's where we kind of went for the idea of his hand. It was ripped off, and he has ties to some criminal underground stuff, so he would have the connections to create something high-tech, and something deadly.

"In the script, there was a chase sequence where there was going to be a weapon involved. So we created something for it that looked pretty normal at first, and then it reveals a deadly weapon as it transforms. The designs I did of his arm were a sonic weapon. We wanted to create something that would show some kind of pulse of energy—to create something that looks interesting and futuristic, but not too out of this world."

■ PREVIOUS **ORTIZ**

■ **FUENTEBELLA**

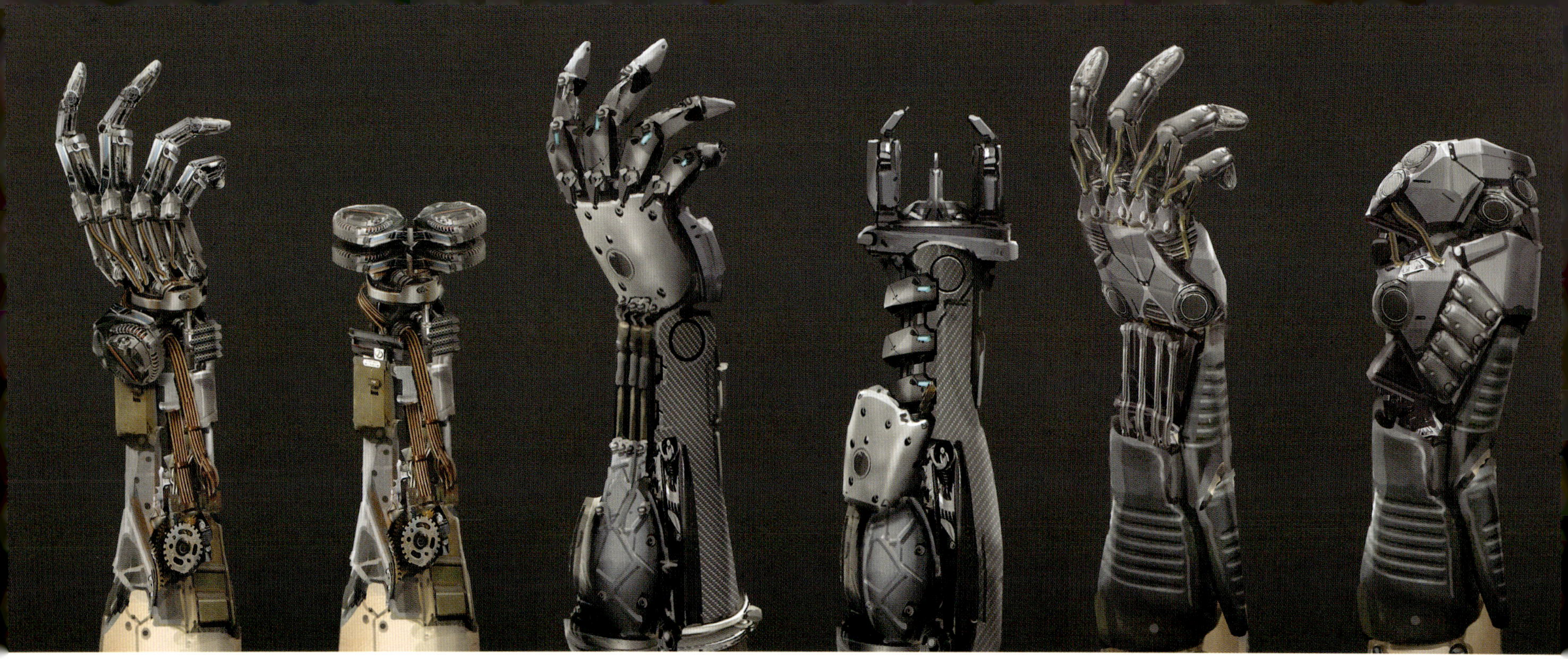

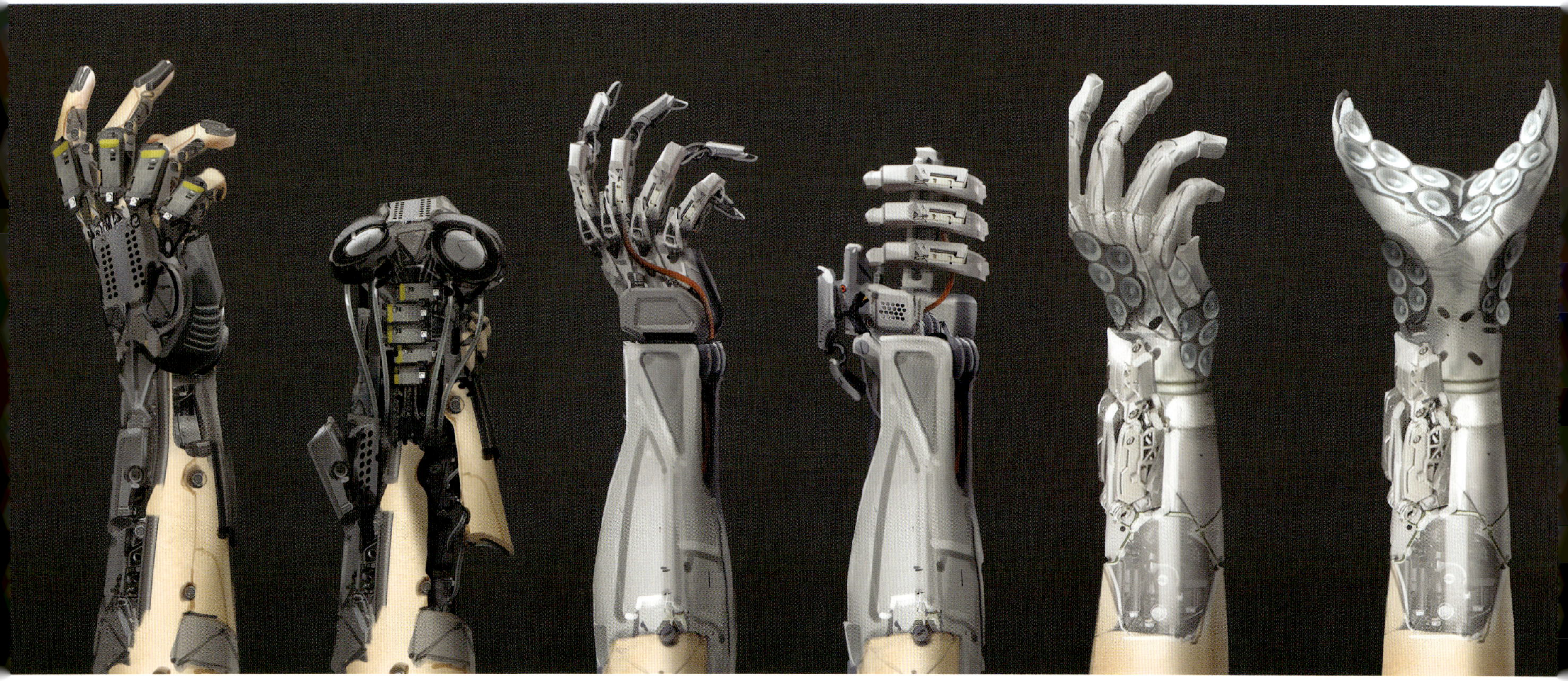

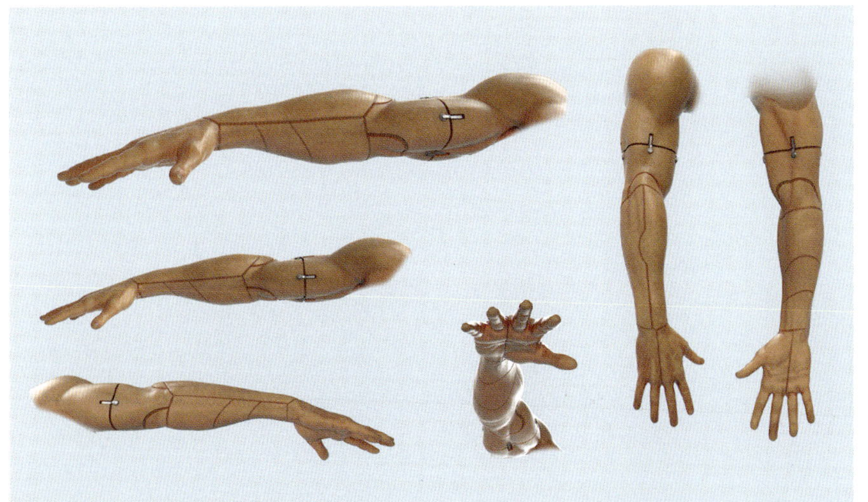

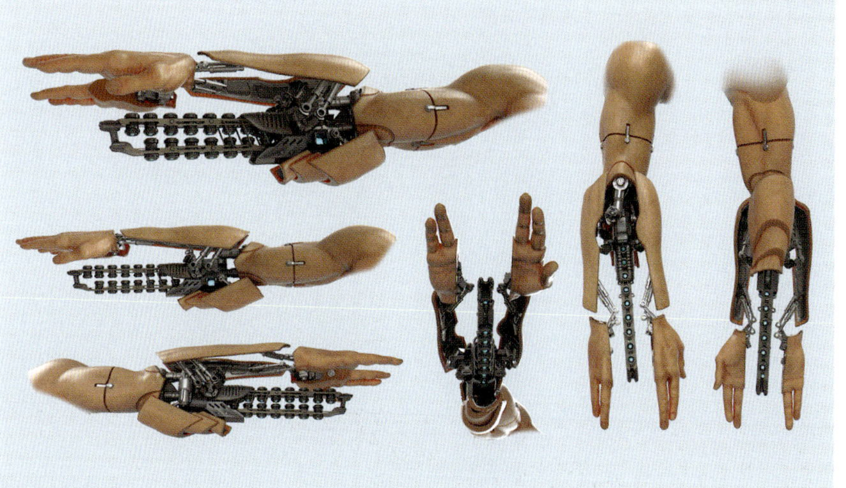

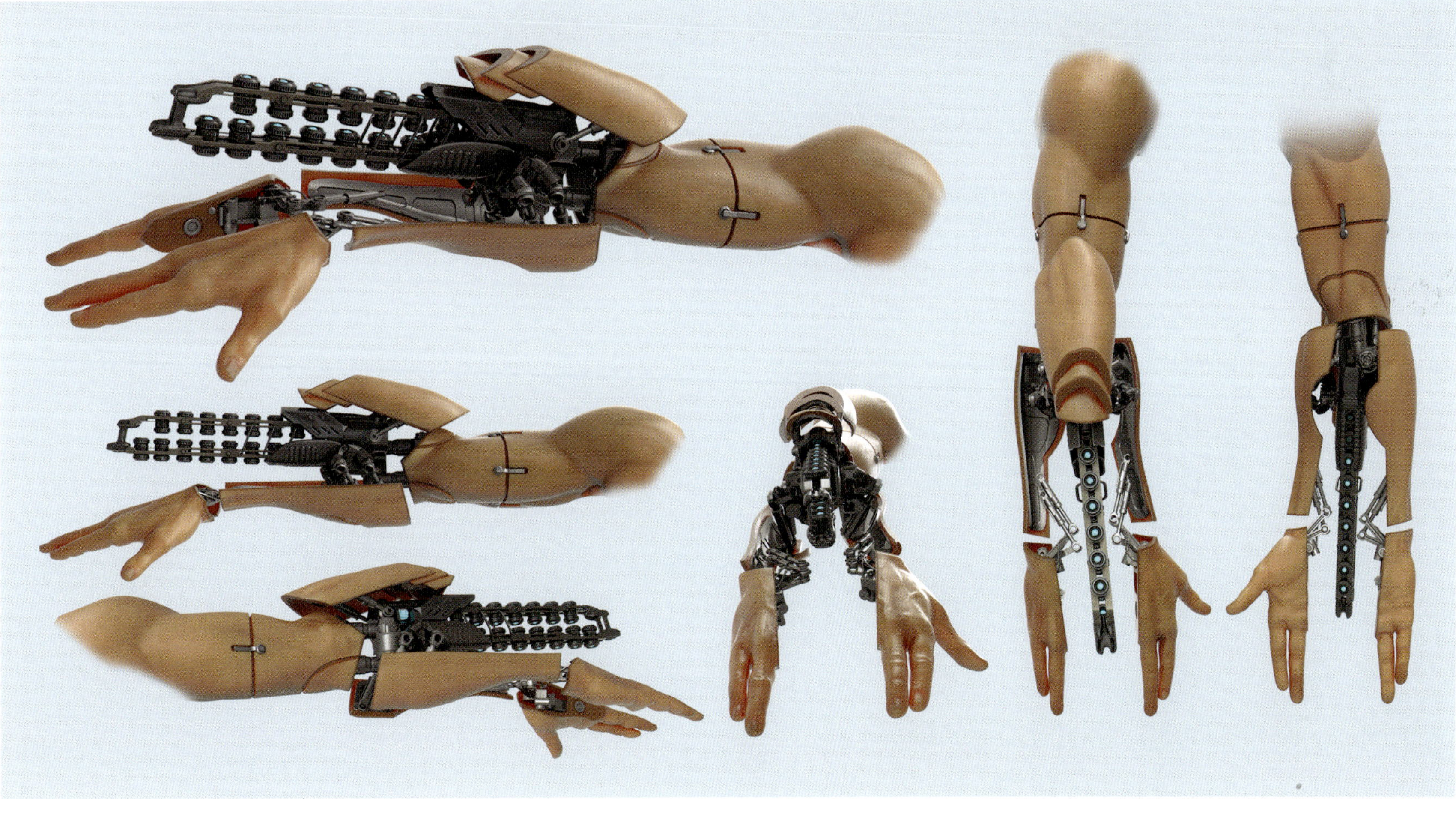

◀ LE

▲ SUMMERS

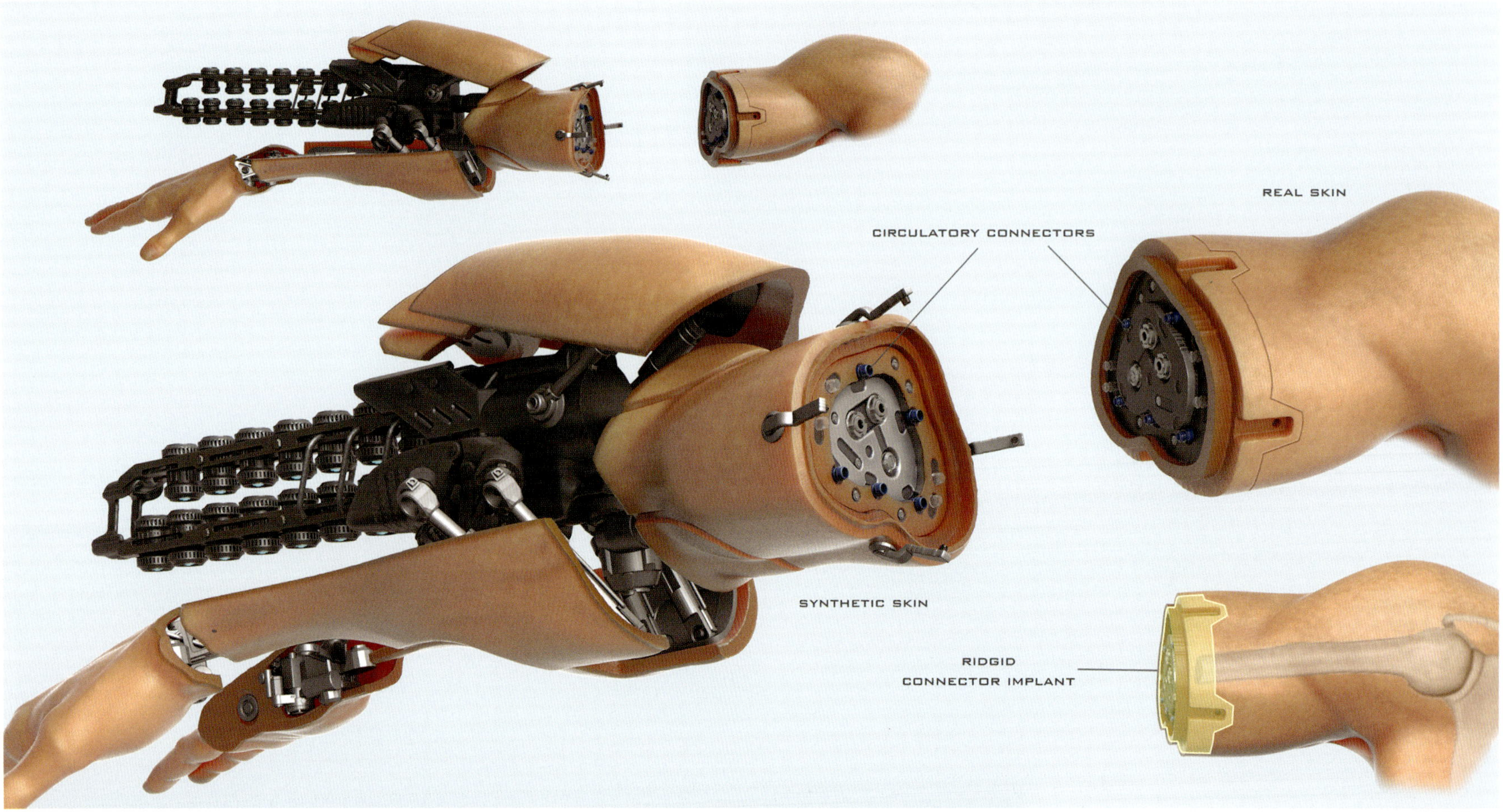

REAL SKIN

CIRCULATORY CONNECTORS

SYNTHETIC SKIN

RIDGID CONNECTOR IMPLANT

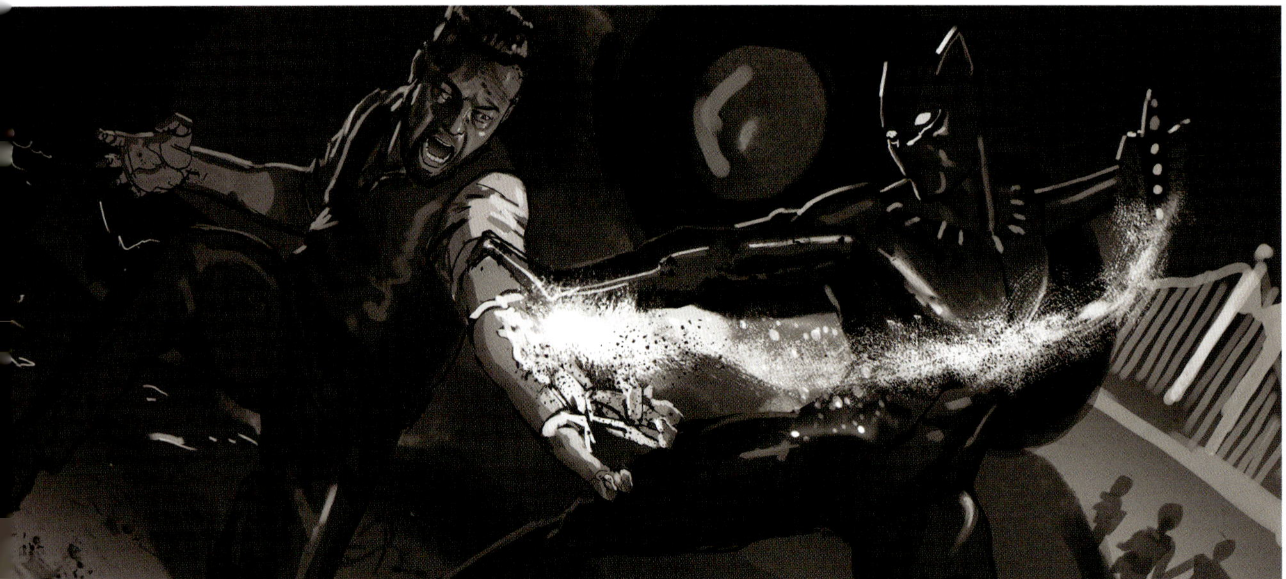

◄ STAUB ■ SUMMERS

"I started designing Klaue's weapon with quick block-outs of how it would look open," Tully Summers says. "Once I found a general shape that I liked, I reverse engineered it—imagined what would have to split, what would have to fold to conceal that shape in a human arm. I thought it would be interesting and make sense to have the arm parts still visible when the weapon was deployed. The intent was to hide the weapon. Once it has been revealed, there is no more need for subterfuge. I wanted the open weapon with its hovering, disembodied parts to feel slightly disturbing, but tried to balance the creep-out factor by designing everything with a clinical, almost medical, sterility."

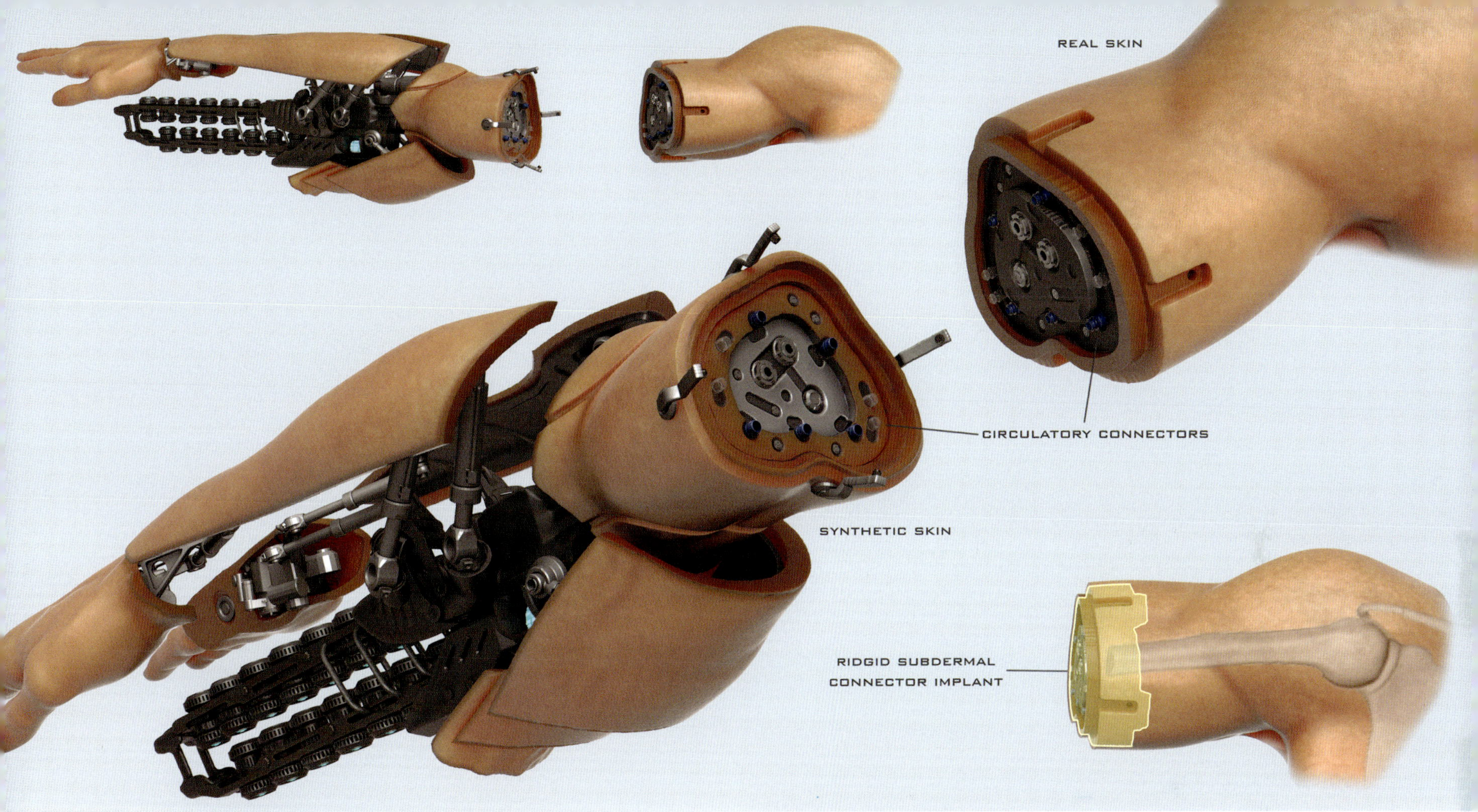

REAL SKIN

CIRCULATORY CONNECTORS

SYNTHETIC SKIN

RIDGID SUBDERMAL
CONNECTOR IMPLANT

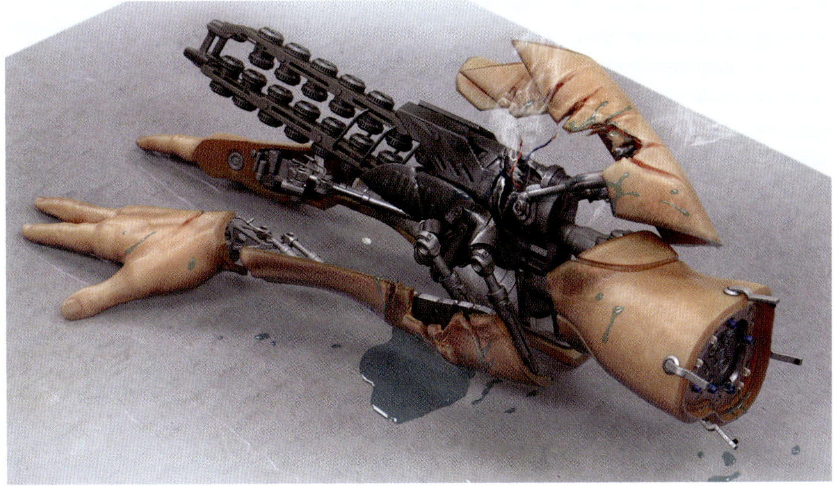

■ SUMMERS

◀ LE

▲ MANDRADJIEV

BATTLE FOR THE THRONE

THE PATH OF ASCENSION

The king of Wakanda is dead, and a new king must take his place. T'Challa, son of T'Chaka, struggles with his sudden rise to power. "He's dealing with the loss of his father on a personal level, but he's also dealing with it on a professional level," Director Ryan Coogler says. "He just got the biggest promotion of his life, and it's a whole nation of people who are looking [to] him for what to do next."

However, T'Challa's birthright in no guarantee. Ages-old traditions must be upheld, and M'Baku, leader of the Jabari tribe, is the first to step forward to challenge T'Challa for the throne. "Warrior Falls is where the king of Wakanda is coronated," Executive Producer Nate Moore says. "This is T'Challa's chance to take the throne, and he has to be presented in front of the nation to allow anybody who wants to challenge him for the throne to come forward. So what he thinks is going to be ceremonial turns into an actual challenge. And when we come back here, T'Challa once again finds himself being challenged for the throne of Wakanda."

WARRIOR FALLS

Warrior Falls, on the river Amanzi Kwakhona Umlambo, is home to the King's Challenge. The contest—in which two opponents fight until one yields or dies—takes place on a small pool ledge several hundred feet below the waterfall's crest. Beyond that shelf, the falls descend into a watery abyss. Evoking the beauty of Victoria Falls in Zambia, it is a stunning setting in which to stage a fight for Wakanda's throne—and its future.

"It's a big set, and we started talking about that pretty much right off the bat," Production Designer Hannah Beachler says. "The whole set is actually industrial styrofoam, and then we plastered over it. The pool has a special epoxy on it for the water and for the fighting because when they go down, we want to make sure that they're not getting hurt. We were thinking about the safety of the stunt people and the actors, so it needed to be a little bit softer. We foamed it, put epoxy down on it, and painted it to look like a rock face on the bottom in the pool.

"The inspiration for it was Oribi Gorge in South Africa, where we spent a lot of time walking and hiking and looking at the rocks and deciding what we wanted that look to be. So we did a horizontal shaling on that. That's something you don't see too often in movie rock. We had such a great team, and it just turned out fantastic."

■ **KUNITAKE**
■ 234-237 **STAUB**, 238-239 **MANDRADJIEV**

■ KUNITAKE

■ **SUMMERS**
■ PREVIOUS **SWEET**

"The idea of anyone coming in to challenge and having to fight is a big surprise with this tradition," Executive Vice President of Physical Production and Executive Producer Victoria Alonso says. "Everyone dresses up, and it's almost boring. As Shuri says, 'Come on, can we get on with this? This outfit is uncomfortable.' So although everyone goes there to talk about the challenge, there has never been one—and then all of a sudden there is one."

One of the centuries-old ritual's traditions calls for the challengers to wear masks: in this case, T'Challa's panther mask and M'Baku's white ape mask. "We had a huge amount of real tribal art and masks as reference," Concept Artist Tully Summers says. "The sheer amount of variation made choosing a specific style for the initial design a challenge. I explored a range, from primal simplicity of construction to more intricate and complex carving and materials. As the King's Challenge masks had to play against each other, I did each exploration of style in pairs, one ape and one panther. We eventually hit on relatively simple skull-like shapes that still reflected the ritual animals. They were further refined to show more of the actors' faces and let the drama of their performance read easier."

■ **SUMMERS**

SUMMERS

Evoking the strength of the Gorilla God Hanuman, the Jabari kings' challenge mask (as worn by Jabari leader M'Baku) depicts a white ape with an aggressive expression—a look that could easily intimidate the fiercest of warriors.

"Warrior Falls is an iconic Black Panther location from the comics that we wanted to bring to life," Nate Moore says. "We thought of a lot of different ways of achieving that. We looked at locations, actually going to Africa to shoot at a real waterfall. And the truth is building it on a backlot allows us much more control with visual effects, with stunts, and with special effects.

"The cast really responds to these sets that are as three-dimensional as possible. It helps them to really inhabit the characters, inhabit the world in a way that feels realistic. If we tried to do all this against a completely blue backdrop, we wouldn't get the same kind of performance."

◀ LE

▲ KOVACS

"I think that Killmonger thinks he's a good guy, which is the best kind of a villain—a villain who actually believes in what they're doing," Moore says. "I think his methods are what make him villainous in that he is willing to cross lines that a hero like T'Challa wouldn't cross in order to get what he thinks is right. But what's interesting is that I think you'll see the audience is going to agree with a lot of Killmonger's ideas, and they're going to be ideas that T'Challa is going to have to take in and actually figure out if he also believes them. So there's a real conversation there that we think is interesting rather than a villain who just wants to take over the world, which is sometimes where we think super-hero movies go wrong."

■ PREVIOUS **SZE**

■ **STAUB**

◀ NIZZI

▲ ROSS

N'JADAKA

Assuming the Wakandan name given to him by his father—N'Jadaka—Erik Killmonger takes control of Wakanda following his victory at Warrior Falls. And as the nation's new Black Panther, he gets a suit all his own. "Because Killmonger was going to have scarification on his body, we were going to try and use that theme in his Panther suit," Head of Visual Development Ryan Meinerding says. "So one of the things that came up for T'Challa's Panther suit is that it's really slick, it's really smooth, and it's a singular skin. For Killmonger's, one of the ways we were trying to differentiate was with the gold representing more of a leopard look, and then also incorporating overstitching so you have bumps that mimic his scarification."

"One of the things that [the filmmakers] were very concerned about was that you knew who was who when the two were fighting in the Vibranium mine because they were both black cats," Costume Designer Ruth Carter says. "They designed a beautiful suit that had very subtle gold leopard spots on it and on the mask itself. It was a gorgeous drawing by Ryan Meinerding's team. It was my job to figure out how to make that. So we used what you would use in any Hollywood shop: a gold, very vibrant leopard suit underneath his cat suit. When the cat suit stretched over this gold lamé, Vegas-y leopard skin, it was like a film over the top of it. It had the appearance of having a special metal that was underneath, like our Vibranium, but it was subtle."

NIZZI

◀ ROSS ■ NIZZI

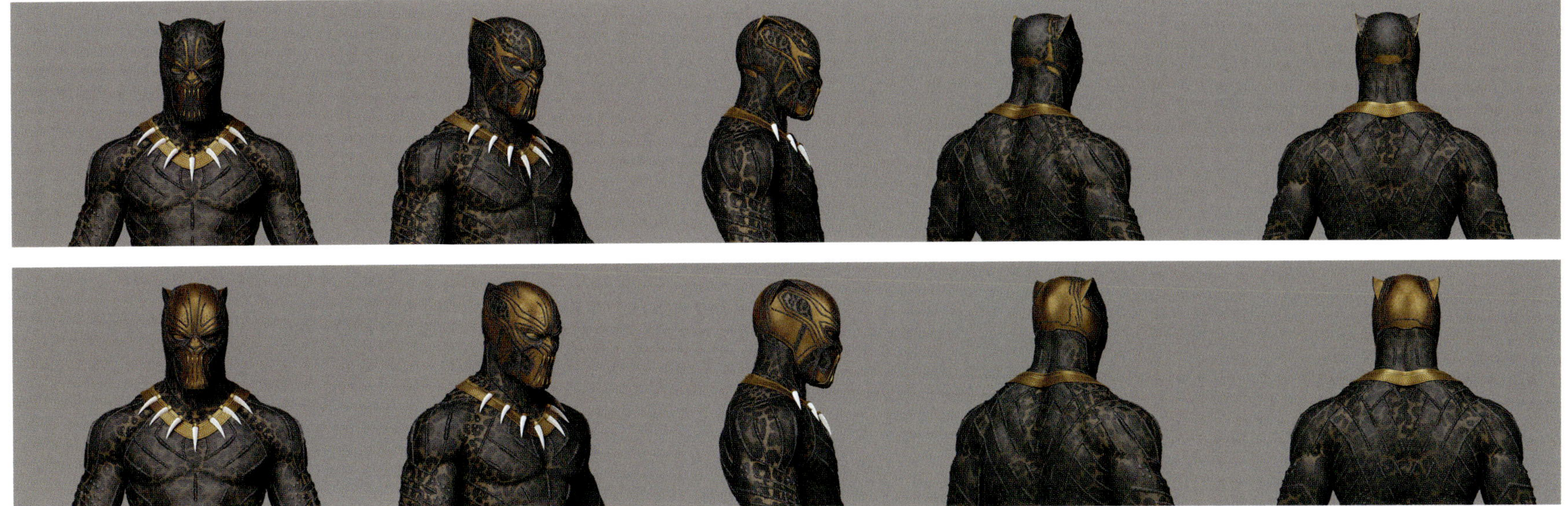

"Sometimes it's necessary for us to create a 3-D model, or sculpt, to fully realize an idea," Concept Sculptor Adam Ross says. "In these instances, once a basic design is chosen, I come in and create it in 3-D so it can then be judged and explored in the round before it moves on to other departments. For Killmonger, two things that were explored in depth were the visibility and color saturation of the underlying leopard print, and how thick and pronounced the scarification details would be on the suit. Since the leopard print had its origins in Erik Killmonger's history in the comics, we wanted to make sure that element was visible, but not so prominent as to be distracting. I tried to make it a very visible element of the suit, but desaturated the yellow so it took on more of an active camouflage look, which was fitting based on Killmonger's paramilitary background. The scarification details were also explored in much the same manner, as they are a reflection of the character's own scarification body art, yet also serve a purpose in the function of the suit. I feel we struck the right balance on both accounts.

"Toward the end of the design process, it was decided to push the gold accents quite a bit further than we had previously. To that end, the bulk of the new gold color was going to be on the helmet. I quickly submitted about half a dozen variations on new gold patterns specifically for the helmet that I felt were in line with codified Wakandan design language, while dialing up the saturation on the suit's leopard print. At that point, everything fell into place, and the final design was approved. I'm really happy with how it turned out! It was a blast working on Killmonger, and remains one of my favorite projects to date!"

■ ROSS

■ NIZZI

NIZZI

"Ryan [Meinerding] asked me to do a shot of the two of them battling inside the Vibranium mine," Concept Artist Adi Granov says. "They only had very early designs of the mine at this point, so I used it for atmosphere rather than just a clear shot of where they were. I just focused on the interaction between the two of them. In the painting, Killmonger almost has this sort of brownish-yellowish panther tone. So T'Challa is like an actual black panther, and Killmonger is almost a jaguar type of design. This concept of them interacting is necessary because it's important to see how they would look together on film."

■ NIZZI

GRANOV ▶

■ KOVACS

■ 270-271 ORTIZ, 272-273 SZE

Part of the Border Tribe's heritage is a close association with the African rhinoceros, generally used to defend Wakanda against foreign invaders. "The rhino was a huge challenge because it felt like everything people did was cruelty to animals, or it didn't make sense for a utopian society to be enslaving an animal for war," Ryan Meinerding says. "So I think the armor ended up feeling like we were trying to make it so they would be obviously protected, but at the same time it also could feel like an enslavement for the animals to be as encased as they were. It's like you're treating an endangered species trivially, which is honestly a concern that I didn't immediately think of when we were doing designs." Ultimately, the filmmakers were able to create a design that respected the majesty of the African rhino.

■ KOVACS

STEPHEN ERIK SCHIRLE

AFTERWORD 2018

by **Ryan Meinerding**

One of the joys of working at Marvel Studios is being part of a team that is creating amazing new cinematic worlds. From the outer reaches of the Nine Realms to the miniature landscapes of the Quantum Realm to the interdimensional kaleidoscope of Doctor Strange, the MCU has always endeavored to take audiences to places they've never seen before.

Wakanda is an extraordinarily worthy addition to this universe. Ryan Coogler's vision for Black Panther's motherland is so full of life and tradition as well as forward-thinking sci-fi, that the country not only becomes a place I want to visit, but also feels as though it has always existed.

The reference file that Hannah Beachler and Ryan created for this movie was a binder six inches thick brimming with amazing source material that spanned not only comics reference, but also incredible real-world cultural touchstones that became the building blocks for the world that was created. Flipping through the pages of this art book, I marvel at the amount of work and care that went into taking so many ideas from that binder and turning them into an entirely new Wakandan culture. Hannah and her team truly delivered a look that respected the ancient tribal roots of Wakanda and allowed them to filter through into the high-tech, sci-fi wonder of the Golden City.

The Visual Development team's contributions mainly stemmed from trying to create a new look for Black Panther and the ***Dora Milaje*** that fit firmly in the Wakanda that was being created, and to create key frames for important story moments in the film. Ryan wanted a sleeker, more advanced suit for Panther that pushed the limits of the tech that we've seen in the MCU. Adi Granov did a fabulous job of developing a new suit for T'Challa that felt advanced and sci-fi, but was also still very much a solid translation of the icon. Ryan had talked about using Brian Stelfreeze's most recent designs for the comics as reference, and we pushed into that direction as much as possible. Anthony Francisco did an incredible job of coming up with a look for Nakia and Okoye that allowed them to look regal, tribal, and fierce, but also place them in an elite and formidable military squad. Tully Summers came up with some truly unique tribal masks for T'Challa, M'Baku, and Killmonger that really helped the Wakandan culture feel like it came from an ancient tradition. Josh Nizzi was the artist who developed the look for the Killmonger Panther suit, and it is a fantastic piece of concept design.

Those characters then merged with all the amazing work Ruth was doing on the costumes for the rest of the Wakandan nation to generate the overall feel of the world. The designs the Costume Department did to create a visual language and history for the different tribes of Wakanda are incredibly inspiring, and I'm very proud to have helped create concept designs that are meant to stand next to them. The collaboration of Vis Dev and the Costume Department is one of the most rewarding parts of Marvel Studios, and Ruth and her whole team brought all of the designs to a level that can only be described as beautiful.

I'm incredibly honored to have been a part of this team, and I have to thank Ryan, Nate, Kevin, Lou, and Victoria for the opportunity to contribute to such a wonderful project. I can't wait for the world to experience T'Challa's Wakanda for themselves!

Ryan Meinerding

◀ **MEINERDING**, *FROM CAPTAIN AMERICA: CIVIL WAR*

■ 278-279 **TAMM**, 280-281 **SCHIRLE**, 282-285 **RIHAL**, 286-287 **SZE**

CONTRIBUTOR BIOS 2018

DIRECTOR/SCREENWRITER RYAN COOGLER is a filmmaker from the East Bay Area, California. In 2011 his student short film "Fig," which followed a young street prostitute's fight to keep her daughter safe, won the Director's Guild of America Student Filmmaker Award, as well as the 2011 HBO Short Filmmaker Award. "Fig" was broadcast on HBO. Coogler most recently directed *Creed*, starring Sylvester Stallone and Michael B. Jordan. His feature-length screenplay *Fruitvale*, based on the 2009 BART police shooting of Oscar Grant, was selected for the 2012 Sundance January Screenwriter's Lab. In 2013, he directed his own screenplay in the newly titled, critically acclaimed film *Fruitvale Station*. Coogler still lives in the Bay Area where, in addition to making films, he works as a counselor at Juvenile Hall in San Francisco. He earned his MFA in Film and Television Production at the University of Southern California in May 2011.

Over the past decade, **PRODUCER AND MARVEL STUDIOS PRESIDENT KEVIN FEIGE** has played an instrumental role in a string of blockbuster feature films adapted from the pages of Marvel comic books. In his current role, Feige oversees all creative aspects of the company's feature film and home entertainment activities. He is currently producing *Avengers: Infinity War* and *Ant-Man and the Wasp*, which will be released in 2018; and *Captain Marvel* and the fourth Avengers film, which will be in theaters in 2019. In 2017, Feige produced *Black Panther*, as well as *Thor: Ragnarok*, which grossed $121 million in its opening weekend and $306 million internationally; *Guardians of the Galaxy Vol. 2*, which opened with $145 million and has grossed over $863.5 million worldwide; and *Spider-Man: Homecoming*, which has garnered over $879 million worldwide to-date. In 2016, Feige produced *Captain America: Civil War*, which grossed $1 billion in global box office and was the year's highest-grossing film, and *Doctor Strange*, which grossed more than $600 million worldwide. His previous producing credits for Marvel include *Iron Man 3, Marvel's The Avengers, Ant-Man, Avengers: Age of Ultron, Guardians of the Galaxy, Captain America: The Winter Soldier, Thor: The Dark World, Thor, Captain America: The First Avenger, Iron Man 2, and Iron Man.*

EXECUTIVE PRODUCER AND MARVEL STUDIOS CO-PRESIDENT LOUIS D'ESPOSITO served as executive producer on the blockbuster hits *Iron Man, Iron Man 2, Thor, Captain America: The First Avenger, Marvel's The Avengers, Iron Man 3, Thor: The Dark World, Captain America: The Winter Soldier, Guardians of the Galaxy*, and most recently *Captain America: Civil War, Avengers: Age of Ultron, Ant-Man, Doctor Strange, Guardians of the Galaxy Vol. 2, Spider-Man: Homecoming, Thor: Ragnarok*, and *Black Panther*. He is currently working on the highly anticipated films *Ant-Man and the Wasp, Captain Marvel*, and *Avengers: Infinity War*, as well as collaborating with Marvel Studios President Kevin Feige to build the future Marvel slate. As co-president of the studio and executive producer on all Marvel films, D'Esposito balances running the studio with overseeing each film from its development stage to distribution. In addition to executive-producing Marvel Studios' films, D'Esposito directed the Marvel One-Shot *Item 47*, which made its debut to fans at the 2012 San Diego Comic-Con International and was featured again at the LA Shorts Fest in September 2012. The project was released as an added feature on the *Marvel's The Avengers* Blu-ray disc. D'Esposito also directed the second Marvel One-Shot *Agent Carter*, starring Hayley Atwell, which premiered at the 2013 San Diego Comic-Con to critical praise from press and fans, and is an added feature on the *Iron Man 3* Blu-ray disc. The One-Shot's popularity led to development of the TV series *Marvel's Agent Carter*. D'Esposito began his tenure at Marvel Studios in 2006.

Prior to Marvel, D'Esposito's executive-producing credits include the 2006 hit film *The Pursuit of Happyness*, starring Will Smith; *Zathura: A Space Adventure*; and the 2003 hit *S.W.A.T.*, starring Samuel L. Jackson and Colin Farrell.

Marvel Studios **EXECUTIVE VICE PRESIDENT OF PHYSICAL PRODUCTION VICTORIA ALONSO** most recently served as executive producer for Jon Watts' *Spider-Man: Homecoming* and Taika Waititi's *Thor: Ragnarok*. In her executive role, she oversees postproduction and visual effects for the studio slate. She executive-produced James Gunn's *Guardians of the Galaxy Vol. 2*, Scott Derrickson's *Doctor Strange*, Joe and Anthony Russo's *Captain America: Civil War*, Peyton Reed's *Ant-Man*, Joss Whedon's *Avengers: Age of Ultron*, James Gunn's *Guardians of the Galaxy*, Joe and Anthony Russo's *Captain America: The Winter Soldier*, Alan Taylor's *Thor: The Dark World*, Shane Black's *Iron Man 3*, and Joss Whedon's *Marvel's The Avengers*. She co-produced Jon Favreau's *Iron Man* and *Iron Man 2*, Kenneth Branagh's *Thor*, and Joe Johnston's *Captain America: The First Avenger*. Alonso's career began at the nascency of the visual-effects industry, when she served as a commercial VFX producer. From there, she VFX-produced numerous feature films, working with such directors as Ridley Scott (*Kingdom of Heaven*), Tim Burton (*Big Fish*), and Andrew Adamson (*Shrek*), to name a few. Throughout the years, her dedication to the industry has been admired and her achievements recognized. In 2015, Alonso was an honoree of the New York Women in Film & Television's Muse Award for Outstanding Vision and Achievement. In January 2017, she received the Advanced Imaging Society's Harold Lloyd Award.

EXECUTIVE PRODUCER NATE MOORE most recently produced *Black Panther*. Prior to that he served as Executive Producer on *Captain America: Civil War*, 2016's highest-grossing film, and *Captain America: Winter Soldier*, which saw Captain America's first solo outing in the modern day. Moore started his career at Marvel Studios in 2010 working on long-lead development and running the Marvel Writers Program, which generated the 2014 smash hit *Guardians of the Galaxy*, among other properties. Moore got his start in the film industry working at Columbia Pictures and Participant Media working on numerous feature films. A lifelong Marvel Comics fan, he is excited to help bring to life the expanding world of the Marvel Cinematic Universe.

CO-PRODUCER AND VICE PRESIDENT OF PHYSICAL PRODUCTION DAVID GRANT joined Marvel Studios in 2008. As co-producer, he recently oversaw production on *Black Panther, Thor: Ragnarok* and *Guardians of the Galaxy Vol. 2*, having formerly served in the same role on *Guardians of the Galaxy, Ant-Man*, and *Doctor Strange*. Additional credits include work as associate producer on *Iron Man 2, Thor, Marvel's The Avengers*, and *Thor: The Dark World*. Current projects include *Captain Marvel*. Prior to joining Marvel Studios, Grant was a freelance production supervisor, having worked on *Fast and Furious, Iron Man, Spider-Man 3, Guess Who*, and *Spider-Man 2*.

CINEMATOGRAPHER RACHEL MORRISON has emerged as a refreshing young talent at the forefront of independent cinema, channeling each story's core emotion into arresting imagery. Morrison has lensed eight Sundance premieres in the past seven years. Among them are the critically acclaimed period drama *Mudbound*, directed by Dee Rees; *Dope*, directed by Rick Famuyiwa; *Fruitvale Station*, directed by Ryan Coogler and starring Michael B. Jordan and Octavia Spencer, and winner of both the Audience Award and Grand Jury Prize for Best Picture; *Little Accidents*, starring Elizabeth Banks, Josh Lucas, Boyd Holbrook and Chloe Sevigny; and *Sound of My Voice*, released by Fox Searchlight. In just one short year, Morrison graduated from *Variety*'s Breaking Through section of the 2012 Below-the-Line Impact Report to being listed among seasoned DP veterans like Roger Deakins and Rodrigo Prieto in the 2013 Below-the-Line Impact Report. That same year, Morrison was honored at the Women in Film Crystal + Lucy Awards, where she was the recipient of the Kodak Vision Award for her outstanding achievements in cinematography. She was also recognized by Indiewire's "On the Rise: 5 Cinematographers to Watch in 2013." She has garnered numerous awards for her imagery, including a Cinematography Emmy nomination for her work on Liz Garbus' *What Happened, Miss Simone?*, as well as an Emmy Nomination for Showtime's *Rikers High*, a documentary about the high school within the Rikers Island prison system. Morrison is based in Los Angeles, but travels the globe to tell stories through extraordinary images.

PRODUCTION DESIGNER HANNAH BEACHLER is a prolific production designer with an affinity for realistic design that emphasizes emotional drama. She previously collaborated with Ryan Coogler on *Creed*, the spinoff from the *Rocky* film series, starring Sylvester Stallone and Michael B. Jordan, as well as *Fruitvale Station*, 2013's Sundance Film Festival breakout, which won both the Grand Jury and Audience Prize. *Fruitvale Station* went on to take home the Prix de l'Avenir in the Un Certain Regard competition at the 2013 Cannes Film Festival, Best First Film at the 2014 Independent Spirit Awards, as well as 44 other nominations and awards. Most recently, Beachler was the production designer on Barry Jenkins' *Moonlight*, which went on to win the Academy Award for Best Motion Picture of the Year and a Golden Globe for Best Motion Picture - Drama. She designed the sets for Beyoncé's visual concept album *Lemonade*, which aired on HBO in April 2016, and for which Beachler received an Emmy nomination for Outstanding Production Design for a Variety, Nonfiction Event or Award Special. In 2014 alone, Beachler designed on three films: Don Cheadle's Miles Davis biopic *Miles Ahead*, which closed the 2015 New York Film Festival and stars Cheadle as Davis; the Darren Aronofsky-produced *Zipper*, which premiered at the 2015 Sundance Film, starring Patrick Wilson and Lena Headey; and Ryan Murphy and Jason Blum's horror remake of *The Town That Dreaded Sundown*, which was released in October 2014. Beachler has worked with many high-profile directors, including Renny Harlin, Peter Hyams, and Gabriele Muccino, and directors of photography Vilmos Zsigmond, ASC, Dean Cundey, ASC, Roberto Schaeffer, ASC, Michael Goi, ASC, and Peter Menzies Jr., ACS.

COSTUME DESIGNER RUTH E. CARTER has an unparalleled ability to develop an authentic story through costume and character, which has made her one of the most sought-after and renowned costume designers today. She has garnered two Academy Award nominations for Best Costume Design for Spike Lee's *Malcom X* (1993) and Steven Spielberg's *Amistad* (1998), as well as an Emmy nomination in 2016 for the reboot of *Roots*. Carter has worked in the industry for over three decades and has been credited with over 40 films and counting. Carter and Lee have worked on over ten films together beginning with *School Daze* and including *Do the Right Thing, Malcolm X*, and *Old Boy*. She is known for her research and diligence to the craft, specifically for her outstanding work for period ensemble films like the highly praised Lee Daniels' *The Butler* and Ava DuVernay's *Selma*. Carter most recently completed work on *Marshall*, directed by Reginald Hudlin, which premiered in October 2017.

PROPS MASTER DREW PETROTTA is a Los Angeles native and a third generation prop master following in the footsteps of his father, grandfather and uncle. A veteran prop master of over 42 feature films, Petrotta has previously worked with Marvel Studios on *Black Panther* and *Marvel's The Avengers* and as well as other genre films including *Green Lantern, Hulk* and *Batman Returns*; the latter as property assistant. His most recent credits include: Christopher Nolan's *Dunkirk, Live By Night, Free State of Jones, Hunger Games: Catching Fire* and *Mockingjay Parts I & II, Transformers: Age of Extinction* and *Revenge of the Fallen, After Earth, Red Dawn, The Rum Diary, The Men Who Stare at Goats, Che: Parts One & Two, Leatherheads, The Reaping*, and *Jarhead*. In 2009, Petrotta was awarded *Movieline* Magazine's "Hamilton Behind the Camera Award," recognizing the achievements of below-the-line craftsmen.

VISUAL EFFECTS SUPERVISOR GEOFFREY BAUMANN is a freelance Visual Effect Supervisor whose most recent credits include *Doctor Strange*,

Avengers: Age of Ultron, *In the Heart of the Sea*, and *Captain America: The Winter Soldier*. Before joining the production side, Geoffrey spent 15 years at Digital Domain with credits on over 18 feature films, including *Oblivion*, *Real Steel*, *Percy Jackson & The Olympians: The Lightning Thief*, *Iron Man 3*, and *Marvel's The Avengers*, among others. Geoffrey's extensive career at Digital Domain prepared him for the challenges faced in today's world of filmmaking, and he has proved this by continuing to excel.

HEAD OF VISUAL DEVELOPMENT RYAN MEINERDING has been active as a concept artist and illustrator in the film business since 2005. Even early in his career, his work was already drawing the kinds of raves reserved for industry veterans. After earning a degree in industrial design from Notre Dame, he transitioned to Hollywood and worked on 2008's *Outlander*. He was hired at Marvel Studios for *Iron Man*, and after leaving briefly to do concept work on *Transformers: Revenge of the Fallen* and *Watchmen*, has been full-time ever since. While working on *Iron Man 2*, Meinerding contributed the design for the new Iron Man armor in the comic-book series *Invincible Iron Man*. He served as Visual Development Co-Supervisor on *Thor*, *Captain America: The First Avenger*, and *Marvel's The Avengers*. He was promoted to Head of Visual Development for *Iron Man 3*, *Captain America: The Winter Soldier*, *Avengers: Age of Ultron*, *Captain America: Civil War*, *Doctor Strange*, *Spider-Man: Homecoming*, and *Black Panther*. He is currently working on *Avengers: Infinity War* and loving every minute of it.

VISUAL DEVELOPMENT SUPERVISOR ANDY PARK studied as an Art/Illustration major at both UCLA and ArtCenter College of Design. His career began as a comic-book artist, fulfilling a childhood dream and illustrating such titles as *Tomb Raider*, *Excalibur*, and *Uncanny X-Men* for Marvel, DC, and Image Comics, among others. After a decade in the comic-book industry, he made a career switch and began working as a concept artist in video games. He was one of the leading artists designing the various worlds and fantastical characters/creatures of the award-winning *God of War* video game franchise for Sony Computer Entertainment of America. Park joined the Visual Development Department at Marvel Studios in 2010 as a visual development concept artist, designing characters and key frame illustrations for *Marvel's The Avengers*, *Iron Man 3*, *Captain America: The Winter Soldier*, *Thor: The Dark World*, *Guardians of the Galaxy*, *Avengers: Age of Ultron*, *Ant-Man*, *Captain America: Civil War*, *Guardians of the Galaxy Vol. 2*, and *Thor: Ragnarok*. He has since become the Visual Development Supervisor on the upcoming films *Ant-Man and the Wasp* and *Captain Marvel*.

SENIOR CONCEPT ILLUSTRATOR JACKSON SZE has worked in advertising, video games, television, and film for studios such as Lucasfilm Animation and Sony Computer Entertainment of America. He is a founding member of the BATTLEMiLK series of art books and is currently a Senior Concept Illustrator at Marvel Studios. He has also taught at Concept Design Academy and Gnomon School of Visual Effects in Hollywood. His credits include *Star Wars: The Clone Wars*, *The Little Prince*, *Marvel's The Avengers*, *Guardians of the Galaxy*, *Ant-Man*, *Doctor Strange*, *Guardians of the Galaxy Vol. 2*, *Thor: Ragnarok*, and *Black Panther*.

CONCEPT ILLUSTRATOR RODNEY FUENTEBELLA has degrees in Design from UCLA and Product Design from the ArtCenter College of Design. Born in the Philippines and raised in San Francisco, he has worked on various projects for Electronic Arts, Atari, Rhythm and Hues, Dreamworks Animation, and *WIRED* magazine, as well as various other entertainment and commercial projects. In film, he worked as a concept artist at Rhythm and Hues before joining the Visual Development team at Marvel Studios. Fuentebella has created key-art illustrations and character designs for various projects including *Captain America: The First Avenger*, *Marvel's The Avengers*, *Iron Man 3*, *Captain America: The Winter Soldier*, *Guardians of the Galaxy*, *The Avengers: Age of Ultron*, *Ant-Man*, *Captain America: Civil War*, *Doctor Strange*, *Spider-Man: Homecoming*, and upcoming MCU films.

CONCEPT ILLUSTRATOR ANTHONY FRANCISCO worked on film and game projects before moving into movie concept art for various effects houses such as Stan Winston Studios, Rick Baker, ADI, Harlow FX and Illusion Industries. Francisco produced art for *Superman Returns*, *A.I. Artificial Intelligence*, *Men in Black 2*, *Spider-Man*, *The Passion of the Christ*, *G.I. Joe: Retaliation* and *The Chronicles of Riddick*, among others. From 2004-2006, he worked as concept artist at NCsoft Santa Monica on the *Guild Wars* and *Tabula Rasa* MMO game titles. Francisco has joined the team at Offset Software as lead concept artist to work on fantasy-based FPS games. In 2010, he worked at Rhythm and Hues on *The Hunger Games*, *R.I.P.D.*, and *Seventh Son*. Francisco also does illustration work for *Magic: The Gathering* and has been an instructor at Gnomon School of Visual Effects, ArtCenter College of Design in Pasadena, Concept Design Academy, and CGMW. He is based in Burbank, where he works on upcoming Marvel titles as part of the Visual Development team at Marvel Studios.

Specializing in Creature and Character Design for film, **CONCEPT ARTIST TULLY SUMMERS** has contributed to *Tomorrowland*, *The Jungle Book*, *Passengers*, *Ghostbusters*, *Guardians of the Galaxy Vol. 2*, *Thor: Ragnarok*, and *Black Panther*.

CONCEPT ARTIST ADI GRANOV works as an illustrator and designer, primarily for Marvel. His most notable works include the *Iron Man: Extremis* series, written by Warren Ellis, and his role as a conceptual designer and illustrator on the *Iron Man* films and *Marvel's The Avengers*. He worked on key character designs and created key frame illustrations for the action sequences. For comic work he is currently under an exclusive contract with Marvel and has produced covers for multiple series over the last few years, as well as a number of short interior stories. Adi currently lives in England with his wife, Tamsin, and their two very weird cats. He likes airplanes, trains, and cars, and his main hobby is working on his 1967 Lotus Elan. He also enjoys beekeeping.

ILLUSTRATOR ALEXANDER MANDRADJIEV has spent 13 years working in the motion-picture industry as a cinematic illustrator. He has worked on such films as *Black Swan*, *Lincoln*, *Edge of Tomorrow*, *Rise* and *Dawn of the Planet of the Apes*, *Philip K. Dick's Electric Dreams*, *X-Men: First Class*, *Doctor Strange*, *Spider-Man: Homecoming*, *Black Panther*, *Marvel's The Avengers*, and more. Mandradjiev is a member of the Art Directors Guild – Local 800 of the International Alliance of Theatrical and Stage Employees working in Los Angeles.

CONCEPT ARTIST KARLA ORTIZ is a Puerto Rican, internationally recognized, award-winning artist. With her exceptional design sense, realistic renders, and character-driven narratives, Ortizhas contributed to many big budget films, including *Jurassic World*, *World of Warcraft*, *Rogue One: A Star Wars Story*, *Thor: Ragnarok*, *Black Panther*, *Avengers: Infinity War*, and most notably her design of Doctor Strange for Marvel's *Doctor Strange*. Karla's work is also recognized in the fine art world, showcasing her figurative and mysterious art in notable galleries, such as Spoke Art and Hashimoto Contemporary in San Francisco, Nucleus Gallery and Thinkspace in L.A., and Galerie Arludik in Paris. She currently lives in San Francisco with her cat, Bady.

ILLUSTRATOR JOSH NIZZI graduated from the University of Illinois with a degree in graphic design. He spent the next nine years working in video games as an art director, concept artist, modeler, and animator on games such as *Red Faction*, *Red Faction II*, and *The Punisher*. Since then, Nizzi has been an illustrator for feature films including *Transformers: Revenge of the Fallen*, *Dark of the Moon*, *Age of Extinction*, and *The Last Knight*; *Captain America: Civil War*; and *Avengers: Age of Ultron*. Recently, he has been splitting his time between his own video game projects and feature-film work.

DIGITAL SCULPTOR ADAM ROSS is the digital sculptor for the Visual Development department at Marvel Studios. His duties include creating proof-of-concept models and sculpts based on the illustrations created by the Vis Dev team, fleshing out rough concept illustrations into finished 3D models, and helping bridge the gap between concept illustration and props/costumes/VFX. He has an extensive background in 3D printing and scanning technologies garnished from a long history in the film, toys, collectibles, and military industries. His film credits include *Iron Man 3*, *Captain America: The Winter Soldier*, *Spider-Man: Homecoming*, *Thor: Ragnarok*, and *Black Panther*.

CONCEPT ARTIST CONSTANTINE SEKERIS has worked in the practical FX studios such as Steve Johnson's Edgefx, Stan Winston Studios, Rick Backer's Cinnovation, Greg Canoms Drak Studios, Quantum Creations FX, Iron Head Studios, and Spectral Motion. On many films from *Bicentennial Man*, *Blade 2*, *League of Extraordinary Gentlemen*, *Where the Wild Things Are*, *Spider-Man 2* and *3*, *Fantastic 4*, *Hellboy 2*, *Hulk 2*, *X-Men: The Last Stand*, *Van Helsing*, and many more. For the past five years he has been a member of the Costume Union, working on films such as *Thor*, *Thor: The Dark World*, *Green Lantern*, *Oblivion*, *Man of Steel*, *Star Trek 2*, *G.I. Joe – Retaliation*, *Ender's Game*, *Thor: Ragnarok*, *Black Panther*, and *Avengers: Infinity War*. He has recently published a book with Design Studio Press called *MetamorFX: Art of Constantine Sekeris*.

ILLUSTRATOR JOHN STAUB is a concept artist and illustrator working in the entertainment industry. He has held a variety of positions ranging from concept artist to art director working on everything from feature films to video games and statue design. His client list includes Marvel Studios, Lionsgate, Sideshow Collectibles, Intel, Sony, and Bethesda. After joining the Marvel team to work on the early stages of *Captain Marvel*, he continued working on *Black Panther* and the upcoming films *Avengers: Infinity War* and *Avengers: Untitled*. Outside of the production environment, John teaches classes at the Concept Design Academy. He currently resides in Los Angeles with his wife and four cats.

CONCEPT ARTIST IAN JOYNER has been working in the industry for over 15 years on a great number of film, commercial, and game projects as well as teaching and giving lectures all around the world. Primarily focusing on creatures and characters, his recent credits include *Thor: Ragnarok*, *Guardians of the Galaxy Vol. 2*, *Bright*, *Saban's Power Rangers*, *Spectral*, and *Jurassic World*, to name a few. When not working, he enjoys spending time with his wife Hilary and their two children, Emily and Alice.

CONCEPT ARTIST STEPHEN SCHIRLE has been a concept artist in TV, film, games, and commercials since 2004. For Marvel Studios, he has worked on *Thor: Ragnarok*, *Avengers: Infinity War*, *Ant-Man and the Wasp*, and *Captain Marvel*.

CONCEPT ARTIST WESLEY BURT hails from a background in traditional art and design, majoring in drawing, painting, and printmaking while attending the Cleveland Institute of Art. He started working professionally as an illustrator and concept artist in 2001 with several freelance jobs with video-game developers and card-game studios. In 2004, he joined the small group of concept artists that would eventually be known as Massive Black, the first-of-its-kind boutique art-outsourcing studio for the video-game industry. Over the following decade with Massive Black, he contributed to numerous video-game titles, toys, and TV and film properties including *Fallout 3*, *Fallout: New Vegas*, *Batman: Arkham Origins*, *Silent Hill*, *Infamous* and *Infamous 2*, *League of Legends*, *Magic: The Gathering*, *Lord of the Rings Online*, *Shadow of Mordor*, *The Sims 4*, and others. He began working on more film productions with the first *Transformers* live-action movie in 2006 and other Hasbro-related titles, eventually working more in-depth on the subsequent *Transformers films: Dark of The Moon*, *Age of Extinction*, and *The Last Knight*. In addition, he contributed work on *Teenage Mutant Ninja Turtles: Out of the Shadows*, *G.I. Joe: The Rise of Cobra* and *G.I. Joe: Retaliation*, and several others. He has worked with Marvel Studios as a visual development artist on *Doctor Strange*, *Black Panther*, *Avengers: Infinity War*, and future films.

ACKNOWLEDGMENTS

Victoria Alonso
Brett Andrews
Doug Appleton
Scott Baker
Geoffrey Baumann
Hannah Beachler
Christian Beckman
Greg Berry
Phillip Boutte Jr.
Richard K. Buoen
Wesley Burt
Ruth E. Carter
Aric Cheng
David Chow
Keith Christensen
Jason Clark
Keenan Coogler
Ryan Coogler
Nick Cross
Matt Delmanowski
Fausto De Martini
Erika Denton
Louis D'Esposito
Patrick Dunn-Baker
Zachary Fannin
Kevin Feige
Bryan Felty
Anthony Francisco
Daniel Frank
Chad S. Frey
Joe Frontirre
Rodney Fuentebella
Sarah Forrest
Adi Granov
David Grant
Joseph Hiura
Alan Hook
Elissa Hunter
Ian Joyner
Carol Kiefer
Vance Kovacs
Tani Kunitake
Fabian Lacey
Percival Lanuza
Khang Le

▲ MANDRADJIEV

Anthony Liberatore
Alexander Mandradjiev
Warren Manser
Jerad Marantz
Iain McCaig
Ryan Meinerding
Dan Milligan
Nate Moore
Rachel Morrison
Zoie Nagelhout
Till Nowak
Josh Nizzi
Karla Ortiz
Andy Park
Jay Pelissier
Drew Petrotta
Avia Perez
Will Corona Pilgrim
Manuel Plank-Jorge
Jacque Porte
Ryan Potter
Vicki Pui
Raj Rihal
Eleni Roussos
Adam Ross
Marco Rubeo
Felipe Sanchez
Alex Scharf
Stephen Schirle
Constantine Sekeris
Steph Semet
Domenic Silvestri
John Staub
Tully Summers
Justin Sweet
Max Sweeney
Jackson Sze
Henrik Tamm
Mayumi Valentine
A.J. Vargas
Bojan Vucicevic
Darrell Warner

ARTIST CREDITS

Hannah Beachler
Pages 12, 28

Phillip Boutte Jr.
Page 54

Richard K. Buoen
Pages 96-103, 106-109

Wesley Burt
Pages 53-55, 134

Keith Christensen
Pages 28, 33, 35, 37, 41, 49, 114-115, 175, 187-189, 191

Fausto De Martini
Page 126

Adam Del Re
Cover Design

Patrick Dunn-Baker
Page 24

Anthony Francisco
Pages 164-165, 172, 174, 178-183, 186

Daniel Frank
Pages 72-73, 77, 80, 145

Rodney Fuentebella
Cover
Pages 92-93, 140-141, 206-209, 213, 215, 217, 219-221, 226-227

Adi Granov
Pages 116-118, 120, 122-125, 136-138, 269

Joseph Hiura
Page 144

Alan Hook
Page 80

Ian Joyner
Pages 168, 176

Vance Kovacs
Pages 84, 86-87, 104-105, 110-111, 169, 253, 274-277

Tani Kunitake
Pages 32, 78-79, 82-83, 150, 240-241, 244-245

Fabian Lacey
Pages 13, 29

Khang Le
Pages 148-149, 151, 228, 232-233, 252-253

Andrew Leung
Pages 62, 66, 202-203

Anthony Liberatore
Pages 7, 32, 34, 38, 40

Alexander Mandradjiev
Pages 28-29, 146-147, 150, 152-155, 158-159, 233, 238-239, 292-293

Jerad Marantz
Pages 132-133

Iain McCaig
Page 223

Alexander McCarroll
Pages 76, 80-81

Method VFX
Pages 1, 296

Ryan Meinerding
Dustjacket
Pages 4-5, 88, 90, 117, 127, 130-131, 160-161, 288-289

Till Nowak
Pages 10-11, 16-21, 24, 42-47, 70-71, 142-143

Josh Nizzi
Pages 128-129, 258-259, 261, 264-268

Karla Ortiz
Pages 56-59, 135, 162-163, 166-167, 173, 177, 184-185, 191-192, 214-216, 218-219, 222, 224-225, 242-243, 270-271

Andy Park
Pages 84-85, 88, 90-91, 130

Manuel Plank-Jorge
Pages 96-97, 100-104

Vicki Pui
Pages 24-25, 42-43, 60-61, 63-65, 100, 104, 143

Raj Rihal
Pages 31, 70, 74-76, 78, 282-285

Adam Ross
Pages 89, 138, 258, 260, 262-263

Brandon Sadler
Pages 1, 67, 296

Felipe Sanchez
Pages 30, 34, 36, 38, 40-41, 50-51

Stephen Schirle
Pages 280-281

Constantine Sekeris
Pages 190, 193, 200-201

John Staub
Pages 48-49, 230, 234-237, 256-257

Tully Summers
Pages 117-118, 120-121, 136, 138-139, 193-199, 210-212, 219, 229-231, 248-251

Justin Sweet
Pages 246-247

Jackson Sze
Pages 2-3, 14-15, 22-23, 26-27, 68-69, 94-95, 112-113, 156-157, 170-171, 204-205, 254-255, 272-273, 286-287, 294-295

Henrik Tamm
Pages 25, 104, 202, 278-279

Darrell Warner
Page 39

◀ SZE ■ 296 SADLER & METHOD VFX